the
trouble
with
theory

Gavin Kitching is Professor of Politics in the School of Social Sciences and International Studies at the University of New South Wales. He is a Fellow of the Australian Academy of Social Sciences and has research interests in the philosophy of Wittgenstein, globalisation, and agricultural development in the Third World. He is widely published, and author of the following books: *Class and Economic Change in Kenya 1905–1970* (1980); *Development and Underdevelopment in Historical Perspective* (1982, 1989); *Rethinking Socialism* (1983); *Karl Marx and the Philosophy of Praxis* (1988), *Marxism and Science: Analysis of an Obsession* (1994); *Seeking Social Justice through Globalization* (2001); *Marx and Wittgenstein* (edited with Nigel Pleasants, 2002); *Wittgenstein and Society* (2003).

the trouble with **theory**

THE EDUCATIONAL COSTS OF POSTMODERNISM

GAVIN KITCHING

The Pennsylvania State University Press
University Park, Pennsylvania

First published in 2008 in the United States by
The Pennsylvania State University Press,
Suite C, USB 1, 820 North University Drive,
University Park, PA 16802

Copyright © Gavin Kitching 2008

First published in Australia in 2008 by Allen & Unwin, 83 Alexander Street,
Crows Nest NSW 2065.

The Library of Congress Cataloging-in-Publication Data

Kitching, G. N.
   The trouble with theory : the educational costs of postmodernism
/ Gavin Kitching.
      p. cm.
   Summary: "A critique of postmodernism and poststructuralism and
an examination of their impact on higher education. Argues that
students influenced by these trends in philosophy produce radically
incoherent ideas about language, meaning, truth, and
reality"—Provided by publisher.
   Includes bibliographical references (p.   ) and index.
   ISBN-13: 978-0-271-03451-5 (cloth : alk. paper)
   ISBN-13: 978-0-271-03452-2 (pb)
   1. Education, Higher—Philosophy. 2. Postmodernism and
education. 3. Poststructuralism. 4. Education—Political aspects.
I. Title.
   LB2322.2.K58 2008
   378.01—dc22
                              2008012578

The Pennsylvania State University Press is a member of the Association of
American University Presses.

It is the policy of The Pennsylvania State University Press to use acid-free paper.
Publications on uncoated stock satisfy the minimum requirements of American
National Standard for Information Sciences—Permanence of Paper for Printed
Library Materials, ANSI Z39.48—1992.

Printed in China by Everbest Printing Co., Ltd

For Frances

Philosophy unties knots in our thinking;
hence its results must be simple
but its activity has to be as complicated
as the knots it unties.

—Wittgenstein, *Zettel*, remark 452

Contents

Preface

'Postmodernism' or 'poststructuralism' has been very fashionable in certain areas of western academia for the last 30 or so years. One of the main reasons for its popularity is its supposed political and social radicalism, a radicalism that has engaged the hearts, as well as the heads, of some of our brightest young people.

I believe, however, that at the heart of postmodernism lies very poor, deeply confused and misbegotten philosophy, a belief that has two important implications. First, that even the very best students who fall under postmodernism's sway produce radically incoherent ideas about language, meaning, truth and reality. (These ideas become even more incoherent when scrambled together to produce broader arguments about the role of 'discourse' in the 'social construction' of anything from society to power to identity to gender). Second, since such notions are often used to support politically radical ideas and causes, their basic philosophical weakness in turn weakens those political arguments—by which I mean that it renders them implausible to an even moderately reflective reader.

In this book, I aim to validate empirically both the beliefs expressed above. To do so, I will be looking at what good students in Politics have made of postmodernism/poststructuralism over the last twenty or so years; what they understand such theory to be; and what they think it commits them to. As its subtitle states, this book is about the educational costs of postmodernism, about the effect it has had on students and the dilemmas it has posed for their teachers. It is not a direct critique of the ideas of

Foucault, Derrida, Laclau and Mouffe or any other luminaries of postmodernism—rather, it is an educational text written by a committed teacher for teachers and students. It uses a detailed empirical analysis of a specific corpus of student work to express and justify an educational worry and concern which has been growing in my mind over the past twenty years—the struggles of able, well-intentioned students to *use* postmodernist ideas, and the less-remarked, but no less agonised, struggles of teachers to help them.

I will show that the efforts of both groups have been frustrated by their failure to come to terms with the philosophical conception of language underlying postmodernist theory generally and its ideas about the 'social construction' of reality specifically. I will explain what this philosophical conception is, what is wrong with it and why, often despite formalistic disclaimers, it leads to deterministic conceptions of the world. I utilise, in a simple and easily comprehensible way, the philosophical ideas of Ludwig Wittgenstein to make this dual philosophical/political critique of postmodernism. I also provide, in Chapter 12, some tips for supervisors and teachers—simple pedagogical techniques by which students' postmodernist confusions can be identified and addressed before they have done too much harm.

I entered university teaching more than 30 years ago. Although my youthful Marxist convictions would not allow me to recognise the fact at the time, I did so with a deep commitment to a classically *liberal* conception of education in which a teacher's primary professional duty is not to tell students what to think but to help them express what they think—whatever that may be—as well as possible. I also commenced my university career with a deep, and consciously recognised, commitment to the classical enlightenment value of the pursuit of truth, something I took to be inextricable from (perhaps even indistinguishable from) the pursuit of justice.[1]

As I reveal in Chapter 10, over those 30 years I have been forced to recognise that the latter—youthful and optimistic—equation was far too cosy and simplistic. Because human beings too frequently lack both wisdom and compassion, they can, and do, use truth to do injustice. I have also been forced to recognise that teaching students to argue persuasively is not at all the same thing as teaching them to argue truthfully. This, however, cannot be counted as a novel discovery. Plato was only one of many to make the same point in his complaints about the Sophists. In short, it turns out that there are profound tensions between educational liberalism and truth-seeking as well as between truth and justice.

However, none of this has weakened my commitment either to liberal educational values or the pursuit of truth, although it has made me more chastened and clear-sighted about both. Accepting the inherent complexities and tensions of these beliefs does not weaken my commitment to them, because only *through* such a serious commitment can I come to recognise those complexities and become (one hopes) a wiser, if sadder, person *and* a better teacher.

However, although *I* remain committed to both a liberal educational ethic and the pursuit of truth, I am no longer sure that the same can be said about the university sector. On the contrary, in a neo-liberal world the university's commitment to truth is being seriously compromised by the stratagems forced upon it to secure funding. In too many cases its commitment to a rigorous educational liberalism is being undermined by the pursuit of an over-facile political radicalism/ethical rectitude.

This book is about one aspect and source of the latter problem or, in a broader context, about a minor aspect of an important problem. For it must be said that intellectually question-begging political radicalism, although the focus of this book, is *not* an especially significant factor in the decline and impoverishment of the university as an institution. That has far more to do with shortage of funds. Governments that deny universities the money they need end up with universities that are not nearly as intellectually honest as they should be. This dishonesty takes many forms (a lot of them swirl around the fetid issue of 'standards') and the one on which this book focuses is neither the most important nor even the most widespread. It is, however, one that tends to damage the reputation of universities in the wider community, and therefore makes it less likely that governments will increase funding on the scale required. Therefore this 'minor' problem is quite politically important and needs to be addressed.

How do I want to see it addressed? My goal, and the goal of this book, is to have intellectually question-begging political radicalism replaced by intellectually rigorous political radicalism. Although some of its individual remarks may appear otherwise, this is *not* a politically conservative book.

Acknowledgements

This book owes much to Wittgenstein and Wittgensteinian philosophy. It therefore seems appropriate to give long overdue acknowledgement to a number of Wittgensteinian philosophers, all of whom have, at one time or another, borne my inexpert intrusions into their field with unfailing tolerance and good humour, and even when they have not wholly understood the background obsessions which were driving the intruder. I would therefore like to thank my friend Nigel Pleasants once again, but also Rupert Read, Phil Hutchinson, K.T. Fann, Michael Nedo, Denis McManus, Ray Monk and Tommi Uschanov for helping me make sense, albeit my own sense, of one of the greatest thinkers of all time.

I would also like to thank David Stern, Bernard Crick and Michael Janover for taking the time to comment on the book manuscript, and to improve it thereby. I owe particular thanks in this regard to Michael Janover, several of whose suggestions for improvement I have incorporated in the final product, to its great benefit. I'd also like to thank my editor, Emma Cotter, for her most careful work, Angela Handley, the senior editor, for her important additional input, and above all Elizabeth Weiss, my publisher, who showed not inconsiderable courage in taking on this odd little book in difficult times for academic publishers.

Beyond all that, I wish to thank my family, and especially Pamela and Sam, who have had, yet again, to put up with the mental disappearance of a partner and father taken up with a publishing project. I also want to acknowledge each and every one of the anonymous student authors without whose work this book simply would not exist. I hope that, even if they do not agree with all the ideas they find in its pages, they will at least approve the spirit in which it is written.

Finally, this book is dedicated to Frances Foster-Thorpe, another former honours student of the School of Politics, UNSW. For if it was reading the work of some of her compatriots that convinced me that Wittgenstein ought to be at least as familiar to students as Foucault, it was she above all who convinced me that outstanding undergraduates *could* grasp Wittgenstein's thought, and that doing so could be as worthwhile and productive for them as it had been for me.

Introduction

In this book, I want to:

■ show that a certain kind of theorising does active intellectual damage to able young people, and indicate precisely what that damage is and how it occurs; and

■ provide a kind of manual by which both students and their teachers may be helped to avoid this damage and to do genuinely productive and rewarding intellectual work together.

My second objective is just as important as the first; the fact that the kind of theory and theorising critiqued in this book has been so fashionable for so many years means that a whole generation of undergraduate and graduate students has been exposed to postmodernist and poststructuralist ideas, and members of this generation have gone on, in their role as teachers, to induct further acolytes into its arcane mysteries. More importantly, it also means that a large number of university teachers in the disciplines of Politics, History, Sociology, Social Anthropology and Cultural Studies, who do not themselves identify as postmodernists, or (indeed) feel comfortable dealing with theoretical and philosophical issues, find themselves required to supervise theses informed by a theoretical perspective about which they may feel not only uneasy, but also ill-equipped to criticise.[1] Moreover, neither students nor supervisors are assisted by the fact that much of the academic literature debating the merits of postmodernism is philosophically narrow, often obscurely expressed and, above all, not well related to the sorts of empirical issues with which students in the humanities and social sciences are concerned.

Theory, Philosophy and Politics

As I stated in my Preface, I believe that the most self-consciously 'theoretical' parts of poststructuralist and postmodernist political theory consist of very poor, deeply confused and misbegotten philosophy.

Quite obviously, any argument to the effect that a body of work is philosophically confused must *itself* be philosophical. This raises the ticklish issue of how I can present my own argument so that it does not reproduce the obfuscatory faults of the literature it is critiquing. How, above all, can I make such an argument readily accessible to the students and teachers with whom I am primarily concerned?

Although I cannot of course offer any guarantees, I believe I have structured this book in a way that maximises its chances of attaining my two main objectives laid out above. This structure is as follows.

Part I, consisting of five chapters, is given over to a detailed content analysis of a sample of undergraduate honours theses, which reveals the deep philosophical confusions embodied in certain uses of language (in particular, in certain metaphors and analogies). This content analysis covers all the most favoured applications of poststructuralist or postmodernist theory made in the theses but focuses particularly closely and critically on arguments for the 'social construction' of 'reality' and 'subjectivity'.

In Part II (Chapters 6–8), I present a critique of the conceptions of language and meaning found in the theses—a critique drawn from the later philosophy of Ludwig Wittgenstein—and show how it may be used by teachers to help students avoid the confusions earlier identified.

Finally, in Part III (Chapters 9–12), I show that these confusions have profound political as well as philosophical implications. In particular I show how and why they weaken the force of the student authors' most revered political arguments, (the 'good causes' of one kind or another that they see themselves as supporting in their work) while being completely redundant to the construction or justification of those arguments. I also offer some practical advice to teachers on how they may improve supervision of theoretical work in Politics.

I accomplish this by using simple analogies, empirical examples and illustrations, so that the entire argument can be followed by the most theoretically unconfident student or teacher. Indeed, one of my hopes for this book is that it will sharply reduce the status accorded to 'theoretical' facility both among those who have it and those who feel they lack it!

Disciplinary constraints

I work in the field of Politics, and have had direct access to a body of undergraduate research work in this field written over the last twenty years or more. I have taken advantage of that access to write this book. Therefore it is focused on the impact of postmodernist/poststructuralist theory on one particular discipline, at one level of study (the undergraduate level) in one university. The book has, in short, a very narrow and restricted empirical focus—a narrowness that allows an in-depth discussion of the body of work concerned, based on extensive quotation from that body. It enables me to demonstrate conclusively that certain fundamental intellectual confusions have occurred *repeatedly* in two decades of undergraduate research dissertations in Politics and International Relations. Moreover, those confusions were chronic and normal (i.e. *not* exceptional or aberrant) in the entire corpus.

I wish to emphasise that, though my analysis is focused on work in Politics, I know from both discussions with colleagues and my own experience as an external examiner that identical issues and problems are also common in the fields of History and Sociology. I hope this book will be helpful to teachers and students in those disciplines as well.

Despite this hope, however, this book is not a substitute for disciplinary-specific pedagogical critique carried out by like-minded colleagues in other fields. I claim in the following chapters that postmodernist theory is, and has been, deeply damaging to many fine students.[2] Such a claim is highly contentious and disputable (and disputed). It is therefore essential that those of us who share this belief proceed beyond rhetorical assertion to evidentially based argument. To do this properly for a range of disciplines in a single text would produce prose so quotation-laden as to be unreadable. If this kind of critical work is to be both reasonably short, readable and directly relevant to the concerns of students and teachers, it must be done discipline-by-discipline, and at a number of levels from the undergraduate to the graduate. I believe that this book is a start and a model for such work, and I hope that it will inspire others to follow its lead.

I now present an outline of the body of student work I shall be critiquing and its place in the Australian university system.

The Australian honours system

Undergraduates in Australia who complete three years of study obtain only a pass degree. If they wish to obtain an honours degree they must proceed to a fourth year of study, and are only allowed to do so if they have obtained a very good average of marks in their first three years. Generally then, the honours year is undertaken by the cream of Australian undergraduate students. As in the English system, Australian honours degrees are graded from first class through to third class. These classes are determined entirely by fourth-year work, and especially by the marks obtained for a 15–20,000-word thesis researched and written during that year under the supervision of a member of staff.

The theses

The dissertations quoted and analysed in this book were selected from the entire collection of undergraduate honours theses stored in my school. My criteria for selection were:

■ extensive and self-advertised use of poststructuralist, post-modernist or discourse theory as their principle analytical tool (irrespective of their actual or notional empirical focus); and
■ at least a distinction mark (75 per cent or better) on examination.[3]

In other words, *all* the theses quoted in this book were graded as very good or outstanding by their examiners.[4] I added this second criterion because I did not wish to be accused of choosing soft targets or of subjecting self-evidently weak work to critical overkill.

The theses analysed date from 1983 to 2006, and there were 253 dissertations in the school collection. Application of the above criteria resulted in 27 [10.6 per cent] being chosen for analysis. Their distribution by year is shown in the following table:

Year	No. of dissertations
1983	2
1989	2
1993	1
1997	2
1998	3
1999	2
2000	3
2002	5
2004	4
2005	2
2006	1

Given that the philosophical issues and problems discussed in the following pages apply to less than 11 per cent of the theses submitted over this 23-year period, am I overemphasising their importance? I believe not, for the following reasons.

'Theoretical' theses of the sort examined here are often preferred by able students, who take their capacity to research and write such theses as important evidence of their higher level of ability. Moreover, this is a view/prejudice often endorsed by their teachers and supervisors, who place a similar premium on the ability of a student to 'do theory'. Indeed students undertaking such theses often expect to attain high marks ('high marks' being defined as a distinction mark or better), and very often do so. Conversely, the majority of students who avoid 'theoretical' thesis or dissertation topics often do so because they define themselves, or are defined by their teachers, as less able than their theoretical 'high-flying' colleagues.

Therefore, because I am concerned in this book with the damaging effect a certain kind of poststructuralist or postmodernist theorising has on some of our most intellectually able young people, the statistical atypicality of this group is not a problem or weakness. In addition, my sample of theoretical dissertations is particularly small because it actually excludes another category of theoretically oriented works—those written in the more conventional 'analytical' or 'Anglo-Saxon' tradition of liberal political theory. This tradition usually traces its origins to Plato and Aristotle, but more often deals with luminaries of liberalism such as Thomas Hobbes, John Locke and John Stuart Mill and such contemporary thinkers as John Rawls, Alasdair McIntyre, Charles Taylor or Jurgen Habermas.

I have excluded this latter body of work because, unlike poststructuralist or postmodernist theory, it usually has no philosophical pretensions. That is, it does not base itself on any explicit epistemology or ontology, or spend time attacking the epistemological or ontological presuppositions of its opponents.[5] Analytical or Anglo-Saxon political theory does of course have *implicit* epistemological and ontological presuppositions (which are often attacked by its 'continental' opponents), but for the most part its practitioners are not much interested in classical philosophical or epistemological issues, nor do they respond to these continental attacks in kind. On the contrary, they tend to skirt philosophy and proceed directly, as it were, to normative or prescriptive arguments about politics and debates on the merits of alternative prescriptions. While I believe the way they do this raises its own important philosophical and methodological issues, they are not the kind of issues I am concerned with in this book.

Quotations

Since my aim is to use the work of 'good' undergraduate students to show the deeply damaging effects of poststructuralist or postmodernist theory, it is obviously important, indeed vital, that I quote their work verbatim and (often) at length. First, I want to show what able students understand poststructuralism and postmodernism to be—i.e., what beliefs and arguments they take such theory to commit them to. Second, I do not want to proceed in a way that can be attacked as 'straw-mannism'. That is, I do not wish to be accused of presenting parodies or distortions of arguments in my own words and then demolishing them.

Rather than include lengthy quotations in the text, each chapter has its own appendix of quotations. Readers will note that some quotations appear in more than one appendix and are referred to in more than one chapter. This is because they provide particularly striking evidence for different, though related, philosophical or conceptual problems. In general, however, I have tried to quote some material from all the theses in the appendices, and to show that the problems I identify in the first five chapters of this book are found, to a greater or lesser degree, in all of them. These problems arise from the use of a certain theoretical perspective, and not from mistakes or misunderstandings in that use made by a particular student, or sub-group of students.

Chapter 4 and its supporting appendices are particularly central to my argument. This chapter, which focuses on the whole notion of 'social construction', is the high point and logical culmination of the entire content analysis in Part I. It provides the rationale for, and leads directly into, the Wittgensteinian critique of the philosophy and politics of postmodernism which takes up Parts II and III.

In Chapter 4, I advance, and try to validate through textual evidence, the following propositions:

■ students see the claim that both reality and subjectivity are 'socially constructed' as the most intellectually original aspect of postmodernist social and political theory, and certainly the one to which they attach most importance; but

- they are often radically unclear and/or deeply ambiguous about what such a claim means or implies to them.

It is important to demonstrate both these points in some detail because I believe there is something deeply philosophically wrong, or at least seriously flawed, in the whole notion of 'social construction'. I also believe that this philosophical flaw is what makes it so difficult for students not to be confused and/or equivocal about its meaning. Explaining exactly what this flaw is, and how it arises, is the central focus of the Wittgensteinian critique of the fundamental philosophical postulates of social constructivism in Part II.

I am especially concerned to bring out certain contradictions and incoherences in the notion that human subjectivity and identity is 'socially constructed'. This idea has been central to the strong philosophical relativist strain in postmodernist thought, a strain that attracts a large number of students. Chapter 8 contains a detailed and critical discussion of the dubious political and intellectual origins of this 'critique of the subject'. A discussion of the political reasons or grounds that attract good students to epistemic relativism, and a philosophical and political critique of relativist epistemology, is found in Chapters 9 and 10.

Despite all this, an advocate or proponent of the arguments and views criticised here may think they are only vulnerable to critique because they have first been parodied or oversimplified by all the student authors. (In other words, that my critique is based on 'derived' or 'second-hand' straw-mannism, as it were.) If, despite this, I can show through extensive and repeated quotation that the views I am critiquing are genuinely held by all the students concerned, and that they are incoherent in the ways I suggest, I will have done something to validate the view I expressed in an earlier book, that postmodernism is 'addling the brains and wasting the time' of some of our brightest young people.[6] More importantly, a close Wittgensteinian analysis of these quotations allows me to show precisely how the confusions arise and (thus) how they can be avoided.

However, because my criticisms of the views and arguments quoted at length in the appendices are so trenchant and far-reaching I thought it essential first to try to obtain the written permission of each student whose work is quoted and, second, to develop a citation system that allows all the students to maintain their anonymity.

It is not my intention in this book to attack or criticise a group of able and conscientious young people, some of whom I have known and taught; still less do I wish to present them as wilful perpetrators of untruths or nonsense. On the contrary, I see those whose work I quote as victims rather than villains. There *are* villains in this story—a few of the principal ones are French, others are American, and some are English or Australian—and I have indeed attacked one or two of the major ones directly elsewhere. The real damage done by the kind of ideas I survey in this book is not felt on those rarefied academic heights where luminaries of the *grandes écoles* joust with each other or their supporters and adversaries from Oxford, Harvard or Yale. The participants in such high intellectual bun fights are well able to take care of themselves. The real damage occurs as a result of the trickle-down of such ideas to lower levels of academe, where they gain students' allegiance more through considerations of status, fashion, political or ethical commitment to some notion or other of 'the good' and sheer undiluted confusion, than anything that can be remotely called rational argument. The aim of this book is to persuade its readers just how extensive that damage is, and how deep a betrayal of the intellectual calling it represents.

ADDENDUM
Research methodology and book structure

I have already outlined how I selected the sample of honours theses analysed in this book, and the universe (all honours theses held in the archive of the former School of Politics and International Relations of the University of New South Wales, Sydney, Australia) from which it was selected.[7] I now want to explain how I sorted and read the theses, before devising the anonymous citation system found throughout the book and its appendices. I also explain the rationale behind the book's structure as a whole.

Sorting and citing the theses

From a reading of the title and synopsis of each thesis, I sorted them into three very broad subject categories—international relations (IR), feminism (Fem) and miscellaneous (Misc). By far the largest sub-group of theses (18) fell into the IR category and they are cited as 'POLS/IR 1–18'. Each thesis in this category self-identified as 'international relations', but the topics dealt with ranged from Australian foreign policy to images of Africa in western discourse, from Russian foreign policy to overt discussions of contemporary trends in international relations theory.

The four theses in the 'feminist' group appear as 'POLS/ Fem 1–4' and each thesis deals, in one way or another, with representations of women in language and/or in other representational forms (the mass media, etc.) There are five theses in the 'miscellaneous' group, which are cited as 'POLS/Misc 1–5'. As its name implies, the 'miscellaneous' group was highly heterogeneous, dealing with topics as diverse as 'postmodern dance', popular Australian cinema, and mass media reportage of the Vietnam War. Page numbers for each block of quotations are appended to their citation numbers.

For clarity of reference, every quotation is given an appendix number as well as a citation number. Appendix numbers appear at the beginning of each quotation, citation numbers at the end of every block of quotations drawn from the same thesis. Thus a quotation cited as '(2.4)' is the fourth quotation in Appendix 2, a quotation cited as '(3.13)' is the thirteenth quotation in Appendix 3, and so on. In *all* appendices blocks of quotations appear in order of their citation number. Thus all quotations from the thesis 'POLS/IR 4' precede those from 'POLS/IR 5' or 'POLS/IR 12', and all quotations from 'POLS/Fem 2' precede those from 'POLS/Fem 4', etc. In addition, I have, simply for consistency's sake, placed all quotations from the 'IR' thesis group first in all the appendices, then all quotations from the 'Fem' group, and, finally, all quotations from the 'Misc' group. As noted above, within each of the three groups, quotations appear in order of thesis citation number; appendix numbers are sequential *across* all three groups. When a quotation, or section of a quotation, appears in the main body of the text its appendix number is provided to facilitate easy cross-reference to the appendices. When a quotation used in the text appears in more than one appendix (as occasionally happens) both numbers are cited.

Selecting the quotations

All of the quotations were selected for their philosophical significance—for what they revealed about the writers' conceptions of language, discourse, knowledge, description, explanation and representation. I did this because more than fifteen years of supervising and examining such honours theses has made me increasingly concerned about their philosophical claims and pretensions, and this was the primary concern of my study. Obviously such passages were found most often in explicitly theoretical or conceptual chapters but, as will be seen from the citations, this was by no means always the case. Generally speaking, an honours thesis of the School of Politics, University of New South Wales, is somewhere between 70 and 90 single-sided A4 pages long and usually divided into 5 or 6 chapters. Overtly theoretical chapters are usually found at the beginning, which means that any and all page references with numbers greater than about 40 are likely to come from the empirical parts of the theses.

In carrying out the study and, even more, while writing this book, I became aware of how similar many of the quotations are. Repetition of very similar quotations from different theses is not only necessary but, in fact, vital to my critical purposes because it enables me to show that the philosophical problems I am concerned with are chronic and widespread throughout the sample, and not simply an artefact of selecting untypical or extreme excerpts, or a few untypical or extreme theses. For the same reason I often quote an individual thesis at some length, to show that the same or analogous errors are being perpetuated throughout an entire dissertation, and are not restricted to a few untypical paragraphs or sentences.

Book structure: Parts, chapters and appendices

The text of this book is divided into three parts: Chapters 1–5 constitute Part I ('Tied in knots: Theory and confusion'); Chapters 6–8 compose Part II ('Loosening the coils: Wittgenstein'); and Chapters 9–12 ('Good causes and bad philosophy') make up Part III.

The quotation appendices already referred to relate entirely to Part I. Appendices 1–3 relate directly to Chapters 1–3. However, partly because of its sheer size, and partly because of its heterogeneous structure, I have divided the mass of quotations supporting Chapter 4 ('The social construction of reality:

Equivocations') into two appendices (4 and 5). Thus Appendix 4 contains quotes concerning the social construction of 'reality' generally. Appendix 5 contains quotes concerning the social construction of 'subjectivity' or 'identity' more specifically.

The final quotation appendix—Appendix 6—supports Chapter 5, and contains quotations from the small minority of theses in my sample that make a clear conceptual distinction between language and discourse, with the latter being defined so as to encompass meaning-laden practices beyond language. I show however that, though this distinction is definitionally set up in the theoretical sections of the theses in question, it is typically not maintained once students put their concept of discourse to empirical work. In all but one case in fact, once empirical analysis commences 'discourse' rapidly reduces to 'language' again. The primary reason for this reduction is that these authors, too, see 'discourse' in the same 'objectivist', 'contemplative' way as the rest of their colleagues see 'language'. And their use of this same underlying 'Augustinian picture' (see Chapter 7 and the addendum to that chapter) of both language and the world has much the same deterministic consequences in their case as in the case of their less sophisticated colleagues.

Readability

I am aware that very heavy use of quotation, however methodologically necessary, can make for very tedious reading. The fact that almost all the quoted material is placed in appendices allows a reader to omit it altogether if s/he wishes and to take my content analysis in Chapters 1–5 'on trust', as it were. Alternatively, s/he can simply read my comments in the quotation appendices while omitting the quotes themselves. Doing so will certainly facilitate an understanding of the content analysis in the chapters, as there is considerable overlap between these comments and that analysis. Indeed in many cases the content analysis is simply a development or deepening of the comments found in and around the quotations.

That being said, each content analysis chapter is replete with detailed cross-references to the appendices, so that more thorough or sceptical readers may readily find the quotation or quotations used to support or validate the analytical points made in the text. I suspect that readers who are predisposed to agree with my arguments and criticisms will omit reading the supporting quotations, while those more sympathetic to postmodernist or poststructuralist theory will, I imagine, wish to reassure themselves that I am not guilty of self-serving selectivity, distortion or parody!

In general, however, I would recommend that *all* readers, no matter what their sympathies, read at least some of the quotations, and especially those in Appendices 4 and 5 concerned with the idea of 'social construction'. I claim in this book that postmodernist theory is damaging the minds and intellects of good students. It is 'in' the quotes themselves, as it were, that one can most plainly see the damage being done, and in that respect they are far more eloquent than anything that I say, or could say, in support of this claim.

Anonymity

And finally, to reiterate a point made in the Introduction, it is of considerable ethical importance to me that none of the student authors should be identifiable to readers of this book (except of course those authors themselves). To this end, both my citation system and my text omit all references to theses' titles as well as to authors' names, and I avoid gendered pronouns throughout when referring to those authors or to their work.

PART I

tied in knots:
theory and confusion

1. 'Doing theory', or creating a landscape

Since the subject of this book is a certain kind of poststructuralist or postmodernist political theory and its problems and weaknesses, we must first ask two very important questions. First, *What is such theory?/How do we know it or recognise it?* And, second (and closely related), *How do students know when they are doing it/thinking it/writing it?*

The answer turns out to be the same in both cases. This kind of theory is both a set of ideas or propositions and a way or mode of expressing those ideas. In later chapters I will examine the first aspect—the most hallowed nostrums or propositions asserted and defended by such theory—and find most of them unoriginal when true, and clearly false when original. In this chapter I wish to focus on the second aspect—the 'theoretical' way, or mode, of expressing ideas. For if students are required to write an opening 'theoretical' chapter or chapters to their thesis and/or to draft theoretical conclusions, they must know how to do this, which means, among other things, that they must know how such chapters should sound, what they should look like on the page. Interestingly, they will never be told explicitly by their supervisors how to produce this sound and appearance. Rather they will simply pick it up from reading theoretical books and articles deemed (by their supervisor or themselves) to be related to their thesis. In short then, the ability to do this kind of theory is picked up largely subliminally and *en passant* as an effect of a certain reading practice. But what is it exactly, in a linguistic sense, that students 'pick up' through this practice?

The quotations in Appendix 1 provide some answers to this question.

The first and most obvious observation to make on the basis of these quotations, is that:

(1)   In learning to do theory students learn to deploy a range of metaphors.

The single-word metaphors most commonly found in the fourteen passages quoted in Appendix 1 include: *matrix, framework, space, flows, domain, machine, system, apparatus(es), bodies, transmit* (and *retransmit*), *network, centres* (and *central*), *subject, subjectivity, sites, location, bases, forces, fields, foundation* and *fragmentation.* Some of the most notable metaphorical phrases include: *process of transformation, create space, transposes movement, movements of desire, waves of ordering, effects of power, mechanism of power, discourse of power, social body, political technology, discourse of identity, sentiments of belonging, model of power, produces power, reinforces power, resistance to power, reverse discourses, counter discourses, local and specific sites, location of power, locate and establish bases, variable forces and discursive fields.*

When collected and laid out in this way it becomes clear, I think, that these are metaphors of a quite distinct sort. What springs most immediately to mind is how rigidly impersonal they all are. Thus, the effect of deploying these metaphors in clusters is to conjure up an unpeopled world of things—often a mechanical or mechanistic world; frequently a world of spatial or geographical things (*sites, locations, bases*). So on the one hand we have a landscape, on the other a kind of technology park or industrial scape. But there are no clearly discernible people moving about the landscape or operating the technology. Of course, there is movement in this world, but it too is mechanically or inanimately produced by *fields*, *forces* and, above all, *power*.

The only even vaguely humanistic references in all these words and phrases are *subject* and *subjectivity*, along with the curiously clashing phrase *sentiments of belonging*. But even here the evocation of humanity is firmly impersonal. The theorist observes (from somewhere 'outside') masses of *subjects* possessed of *subjectivity* who experience, among other things, *sentiments of belonging*. But who precisely these subjects are we do not know—they certainly do not include the theorist, about whose subjectivity we are told nothing, and whose sentiments (whether of belonging, or anything else) are never revealed.

There is more to it than this, because we do not merely learn nothing of the theorist as a subject from these metaphors. Rather,

(2) One of the main functions or effects of these metaphors is to remove the theorist as writer or author from the discourse—to make the theorist as writer disappear.

It will be readily apparent that in all the quotations in Appendix 1, in fact in virtually all the quotations in all the appendices, first-person pronouns and forms of the verb are entirely absent. In short, there are no 'I think's, 'I feel's, 'it seems to me's etc., let alone any openly introspective or reflexive passages. This form of theoretical prose is, in short, rigidly objectivist, both in the sense that it conjures up a world of objects affected or moved only by mechanical or inanimate forces, but also in the sense that the prose itself appears to have no subject or creator. It itself is an object produced by some kind of 'automatic' or 'mechanical' process (precisely the process of 'theorising'). We shall investigate the deep significance of this latter point in Chapter 6.

This second prosaic characteristic of theory—its rigid objectivity and impersonality—is no accident. On the contrary, as we shall discover in Chapter 9, nearly every major exponent of poststructuralist and postmodernist theory was and is deeply hostile to what Althusser calls 'the problematic of the subject'. Indeed one of the central theoretical postulates of postmodernism is that 'subjects' and 'subjectivities' are 'socially constructed' or 'constructed in discourse'. I will discuss this contention as it is understood by the student authors in Chapter 4. For the moment I wish only to note that, in following this hostility to any 'essential' (as it is put) subjectivity consistently through into its very form of prose,

(3) postmodernist theory leaves the epistemological status of the metaphors employed in it radically unclear.

That is, are we to understand words such as *matrix, framework, system, flows, forces* or *structure*, or phrases such as *transposes movement, movements of desire* or *variable forces and discursive fields* as metaphors, or are we to take them as names of real objects and forces? If we take them as metaphors then we would take a proposition such as 'Prisons and punishment structures have become a spectacle and performance of power for the government' (1.6) as a way of talking/writing about what *prisons and punishment structures* do—a way that could (presumably) be replaced by another way of talking/writing employing (presumably) different metaphors without losing descriptive accuracy or analytical acuity. If, however, we take *spectacle* and *performance of power* to be names of real objects and processes, then (presumably) these are not 'mere' metaphors, readily replaceable by functional synonyms, but rather the objectively correct characterisations of prisons and punishment structures revealed by 'theory' (or some such). However,

(4)   in removing or occluding any authorial subject, 'theoretical' prose tends to bias or weight the epistemological choice above strongly in favour of the second 'realist' alternative.

To ask 'Why are we/you deploying these metaphors?' or 'Why don't we/you deploy these alternative metaphors or descriptive techniques?' I must postulate a 'we' or 'you' to whom these questions are addressed and who faces, or has, this choice. But if there is no authorial subject present then the reader (and the writer?) is, at the very least, strongly encouraged to suppose that what theorists are doing *is* 'characterising' or 'identifying' real (but hidden?) objects and forces 'out there' in society, and not just deploying metaphors. In fact, removal or occlusion of the author tends to leave both reader and writer, by default as much as by anything else, with a conception of theorising in which theory becomes a 'reflection' or 'picture' of the real. To put all that more simply, if nobody is writing this theory, then reality must be writing it (albeit 'through' or 'by means of' the theorist).

One further point: in English, indeed in all Indo-European languages, 'proper' sentence structure requires every sentence to have a subject (doer, mover, thinker, actor) and a predicate (the done to, the moved, the thought about, the acted upon).[1] As theoretical prose systematically excludes personal subjects, this means that

(5)   it becomes functionally or grammatically necessary to put abstractions in subject positions in many or most theoretical sentences.

Thus, we see: 'constructivist theory can account for' (1.1); 'the theoretical framework of constructivism has made provisions for' (1.1); 'this theory fails to see the important role that' (1.2); 'I do not contend that Chinese culture cannot think causally, nor that Australia cannot think in terms of "tendency"' (1.3); 'this framework presumes' (1.4); 'International relations theory functions to create . . .' (1.6); 'knowledge and power relationships constitute . . .' (1.6); 'Society not only becomes involved in . . .' (1.8); 'security deploys a discourse of . . .' (1.9); and 'power relations function in the construction of truth' (1.10).

Grammatically, there is nothing particularly wrong with this practice. All writers of English (and French, Spanish and German) give abstractions subjective powers sometimes. (Readers will find many examples in this book.) But when the technique is deployed as frequently and unremittingly as it is in this kind of theoretical discourse then the issue of whether people use language or language uses (and indeed 'constitutes' or 'constructs') people tends to be prosaically foreclosed—foreclosed by its very prose form—in favour of the latter. The question of whether the social or indeed linguistic 'construction' of identities is philosophically coherent will be discussed at length in Chapter 8. Here I simply want to note that when students learn to read and write this kind of theoretical prose, they also learn to deploy a prose that has a quite specific—and problematic—philosophical conception built in to it. They think they are just learning to 'do theory', but in fact they are simultaneously learning to reproduce a philosophical conception of the world that is partially (only partially) 'validated' in that prose form itself. Do abstract social forces rule people? *Certainly* they do in the prose world of 'theory'!

2. 'Relationships', or arranging objects in the landscape

One of the logically inevitable concomitants of a metaphorical conception of theory as a landscape or space filled with a variety of abstract objects is that putting theory to work empirically will consist in large part of describing or characterising the relationships that exist between and among these objects. English in particular is a language with an *immense* relationship vocabulary, so it is possible to describe such relationships in very tight, constraining or determining ways, or in very loose, vague or uncertain ways. In other words, it is possible to fill this space or landscape with causal or mechanical relationships, in which some objects are pushed and pulled about haplessly by other objects that *determine, structure* or (even) *cause* them. But it is also possible to fill the space with a kind of metaphorical mist or smoke in which objects (perhaps, indeed often, the same objects) *influence, modify, enable, form, render, limit, have a part to play in* or *make a difference to* other objects. Thus when the conceptual mist lifts things have definitely changed, even if one is not quite sure how or why. Or, to put that more directly, when deployed in the conceptual space of 'theory', the immense richness and variety of English relationship vocabulary can allow for significant degrees of ambiguity, equivocation or (even) self-contradiction. In particular it can allow highly deterministic formulations to be advanced, reiterated, partially withdrawn and qualified, and then reiterated again, often within a single page or even paragraph. In the quotations in Appendix 2 we can see this happening.

POLS/IR 17 in particular (2.3–2.12) poses the issue very clearly. What, precisely, is its author saying about language or discourse? Is s/he saying that language or discourse *causes* or *determines* (in and of itself, as it were) what its users will think, feel and do in the world, or is s/he saying that it is, say, an important influence on these things, but not a totally exclusive or determining one? The web of theoretical metaphors s/he has woven makes it very difficult for a reader to decide. More importantly, it seems to make it very difficult for the author to decide. Indeed there are paragraphs, even single sentences, containing formulations that 'point both ways', as it were.

Thus, his/her very first proposition about 'discourse' says 'The power of discourse—the way it can determine (alter, constrain, enable) the way an issue is conceived' (2.3/6.2). But 'alter', 'constrain' and 'enable' are certainly not synonyms for determine. Constrain comes nearest (at least, if we give determine its stricter mathematical meaning), but the verbs 'alter' and 'enable' suggest a very different relationship.

Having equivocated in his/her very first attempt to define discourse, the author carries that equivocation through his/her entire analysis. The paragraph beginning (trenchantly), 'In effect discourse produces the world...' (2.6) provides a particularly rich example of the way in which highly deterministic propositions are followed rapidly by diluting or qualifying formulations simply by changing the 'relationship-specifying' verbs. Thus the author's characterisations of the 'relationship' between discourse and its effects or consequences for human thought and action are (in order): *produces, renders, shapes and changes, determines, inevitably leads, makes possible, excludes, produces* (again), *shape* (again), *influence, have enormous influence* and *legitimise.*

The subsequent quotations from the same text confirm that this explanatory equivocation continues through the empirical sections of the thesis (which are concerned with the Australian government's policies towards asylum seekers and their official justification through the rhetoric of security). At times the author writes as if once this rhetoric was established and publicly promulgated by the government it determined both popular perceptions of asylum seekers and popular support for the policies. At other times, however, it seems to be suggested that, while this rhetoric *played an active and key role* or even *had an enormous impact* it was not exclusively determining of these other things (2.7–2.12). (Even the more qualified formulations are weakened by the author's failure to suggest what factors or forces—other than discourse—might have been at work.)

Having worked through this example, readers will quickly identify the similar equivocations afflicting POLS/IR 15, POLS/IR 18 and POLS/Fem 3.

The quotations from POLS/IR 18 (2.17–2.20) demonstrate a similarly eclectic range of relationship-specifying verbs and verb phrases from *determines, construct* (three times), *constructed as* (twice), *produces only, prescribes the terms, pre-determined* (*subject positions*) and *forecloses discussion*—at the more deterministic end—to *constrains, restricts the scope, modifies, shapes, imposes limits* and *situated within* at the less deterministic end. Similarly, in POLS/IR 15 (2.1–2.2) and POLS/Fem 3 (2.21–2.24) we find, often in the same sentences or paragraphs, *determine, play a part* (2.2); *position, shape, implicate, produce, provide, make intelligible, contest, produce* (again) and *reinforce* (2.21–2.24). And in all these cases, the effect is that students are allowed, or more accurately allow themselves, both to have their deterministic cake and eat it (or perhaps regurgitate it).

3. Zapping landscapes and setting objects alight: *Power*

The two previous chapters have suggested that a writer who creates a theoretical space or landscape full of objects but entirely devoid of people (except in the abstract form of 'subjects' and 'subjectivities') can only 'dynamise' that landscape or space—make something happen in it—by using abstractions (abstract nouns) as both active subjects and acted-upon predicates in descriptive and explanatory sentences and propositions. The writer does this by using a wide variety of verb forms to specify the different 'relationships of effect' between the objects in the landscape.

However, one particular variety of postmodernist theorising—that primarily influenced by the work of Michel Foucault—uses another dynamising 'force' to set the theoretical landscape of human society in motion: *power*!

Foucault's very particular conception of power is uniquely well fitted for this dynamising role—to bring a reified world of objects alive—because of its radically 'de-centred' and indeed 'omnipresent' 'structure'. To use a phrase that often appears in discussions of Foucault's work (and which indeed appears in one of the quotations in Appendix 3), for Foucault *power is everywhere* (3.8). This means that: in the theoretical landscape it is transmitted from the valleys as well as from the mountains; found humming in the villages as well as in the cities; and dynamises the poor and oppressed subjects and subjectivities as well as the rich and powerful ones. Student evocations of Foucault's notion of power are often replete with metaphors and analogies drawn from electricity generation and transmission and from the universe of electromagnetism: *the power network* (3.7); *mobile and transitory points of resistance* (3.7); *discourse transmits and produces power* (3.11); *power through domination produces greater possibilities for resistance by subjects* (1.12/3.12); *where are the sites for resisting it located?* (1.12/3.12); and *identity is produced through variable forces and discursive fields* (3.15).

But—and this is the crucial point—whereas in a modern or even postmodern landscape, power, even electrical power, operates only to 'dynamise' a set of objects already in existence, in Foucault it is this power—the omnipresent power of discourse— that actually *creates* that social landscape. The power of discourse actually constructs . . .

But constructs *what*? That is the question. And here we are faced by precisely the same epistemological choice considered in Chapter 1. That is, are we to say that discourse constructs human society itself or that it constructs the understandings of society (at least, the dominant understandings) held by those 'subjects' who live within it? Or (a question for detailed consideration in Chapter 4) are these two things ultimately the same thing?

Once again, the student authors' answers to this crucial question are themselves crucially ambivalent or ambiguous. And discussing why this is produces some interesting insights into the constraints imposed by the theoretical metaphors being used.

Two of the theses quoted in Appendix 3 (POLS/IR 5 and POLS/ Fem 2) quote, in whole or part, the following passage from Steven Lukes' book *Power* (Blackwell, 1986), which briefly outlines Foucault's conception of power.

In a society such as ours, but basically in any society, there are manifold relations of power which permeate, characterise and constitute the social body, and these relations of power cannot themselves be established, consolidated nor implemented without the production, accumulation, circulation and functioning of a discourse. (3.1 and 3.9)

This passage is deeply ambiguous. It first asserts that 'in any society there are manifold relations of power' (which certainly sounds as if, in some sense, the 'society' pre-exists the 'relations of power'); but *then* says that 'those relations of power cannot . . . be established without . . . discourse' (which certainly sounds as if the 'discourse' pre-exists the 'society' or, at least, its 'relations of power').

Many similar passages in the theses themselves are ambiguous in exactly analogous ways. Thus a passage from POLS/Fem 2 asserts that 'Power . . . is a dynamic situation that is immanent and continually exercised within the complex relations of individuals and society' (3.8). This certainly *sounds* as if these 'individuals' and 'complex social relations' pre-exist the 'power', but the thesis also reproduces the quotation asserting that 'Power exists in "manifold relations(s) . . . which permeate, characterise, and constitute the social body . . ." ' (3.9)—so perhaps not!

Furthermore, the same student author claims that Foucault's 'subjects themselves exercise power' (which certainly sounds as if the said subjects pre-exist the said power). But they are also *characterised* by such power, indeed *constituted through* it, 'such that the exercise of power does not require external surveillance or coercion' (3.10).

This last contradiction raises a political issue for the author of POLS/Fem 2, as it does for many other readers of Foucault. The reason for this is that 'while he [Foucault] claims that subjects are normalised, "responsibilised" and disciplined through the dynamics of power relations, he also asserts that individuals are subjective, autonomous agents' (3.14). So 'Foucault seems to be implying that individuals are animated but yet autonomous within discursive power. Through voluntary self-regulation and self-discipline they achieve and secure a subjective identity. So, we are subjected to power, but also autonomous within it? Foucault introduces this contradiction to allow for his all important possibility of resistance. However, it is a contradiction that Foucault neglects to resolve adequately, and one that causes feminists to question the lack of a normative framework for resistance' (3.14).

I will discuss the real ontological issues here at length in the next chapter, which focuses explicitly on the idea of the social construction of reality. It is worth noting, however, that there is also a more narrowly linguistic issue at play, an issue produced by (or rather 'in') my primary concern in these first three chapters—the dominant or over-determining metaphor of a theoretical space or landscape filled with (mainly inanimate) abstract objects.

The problem is this. Given the linear structure of any narrative (i.e., the necessity to put some words before others) it is very difficult to say simultaneously that discursive power enters, zaps or dynamises the landscape and all the objects within it and makes, creates or constructs the landscape and all the objects in it. That is, one is linguistically constrained to say either that the landscape and objects are 'there' first (and the power comes along to dynamise it/them afterwards), *or* that the power is 'there' first (and somehow 'produces out of itself' the landscape and objects afterwards).

That is to say, anything that happens in a landscape or space, even if it happens rather quickly (a lightning strike or an electrical discharge, for example) has to occur in time, and has to take time, so questions of temporal order necessarily arise.

The philosophical issue, however, is whether this is just a linguistic problem—one signalling, perhaps, the limitations of this particular set of metaphors—or whether the linguistic problem is signalling a more important ontological difficulty. That is, is the problem just that it is impossible to *say* simultaneously that people both use discourse and are constructed by it, or that they both use power and are constituted by it? Or is this a signal that one is trying to say something substantively incoherent, where incoherent means something like 'not, when closely examined, compatible with any actual or imaginable human reality that we know'?

As noted, I will return to this question in Chapter 4, but I want to make one relevant historical observation here. Empirical evidence tells us that the human species existed for a long time before *homo sapiens* could speak, or use language. At the very least this must put some absolute historical limits on the proposition that (human) social reality is socially constructed or constructed in discourse (although we may not be able to say much about those ancient limits or what lay beyond them).

4. The social construction of reality: Equivocations

It is time to approach the philosophical heart of matters, but before doing so I want to summarise my analysis so far.

As students learn to do poststructuralist or postmodernist theory they learn to deploy a set of metaphors—metaphors that create a curious, alienated world or landscape in which there are 'relations of effect' between and among a variety of abstract, impersonal objects—relations that are often represented in impersonal mechanical, geometrical and 'physical force' ways. The only people in this landscape are 'subjects', possessed of 'subjectivity', but these subjects only appear anonymously and *en masse* and their subjectivity is presented, ultimately, as an effect or creation of 'discourse'. This raises the ticklish question of whether, or to what extent, the social landscape pre-exists the discourse or the discourse the landscape. But, following the lead of the theorists they admire, all the student authors see this as somehow being a 'relationship of simultaneity'. In other words, their basic epistemological and ontological postulate is that there is no social landscape that is not 'constructed' in the discourse of subjects, but simultaneously there are no social subjects whose 'subjectivity' is not in itself a social effect of inter-subjective discourse.

This chapter deals with both these forms of alleged 'social construction', i.e., of social reality and of social subjects. As we will see, the philosophical problems of the latter are really only a sub-set of the former, although they raise certain issues of self-contradiction rather more acutely. For clarity of presentation, however, I have subdivided the chapter's quotations into two separate appendices. Those concerned with the social construction of reality more generally are grouped together in Appendix 4; those concerned specifically with the social construction of subjectivity are in Appendix 5. Because the philosophical problems and issues that arise are often expressed in the detail (and in the implicit contradictions) of the quotations, in both appendices my comments are closely interleaved with the quotations themselves. I have done this to bring out these contradictions 'immediately' for the reader and facilitate reference back and forward from the pages that follow, because many (though not all) of my comments in the appendices are taken up again and elaborated in the chapter analysis. To make them clearly distinct from the quotations, my comments appear in a **bolder typeface**.

As will be seen from my comments in Appendices 4 and 5, I do not deny propositions such as *reality is socially constructed* or *subjectivity is socially constructed*, but neither do I endorse them. Rather I am continually struck by the way in which both claims combine portentousness and vagueness in almost equal parts. Thus it is very difficult either to endorse *or* deny them because it is so difficult to know precisely what they mean.

Let us take the portentousness first.

'There are no facts, no proper meaning to words, no authentic vision of a text, in short no simple truths.' (4.6)
'Such texts . . . can create not only knowledge but also the very reality they appear to describe.' (5.2)
'. . . knowledge (or meaning) is not determined by reality,

or fixed in convention, but is rather a constructed product of power relations.' (4.17)

'Power and knowledge are mutually constitutive. Truth is a function of power.' (3.1/4.5)

'Language does not simply refer to reality; it *constructs* reality.' (2.16/4.19)

'There is no pre-discursive gender or sex.' (5.17)

'Prior to the call, there is no social subject.' (5.25)

'There *is* no "reality" accessible to us outside thought; an object has existence, but not one meaning which constitutes its reality. What gives an object reality is our thought, our "knowing" of it. We endow "reality" through "naming" and we cannot name or know in this sense, outside of a discursive structure.' (4.21/6.5)

'in the same way as we understand the earthquake, we can only understand the material ritual, for example, of a lecture, within the discourse of "the modern university" referred to earlier.' (4.21/6.5)

'all institutional arrangements . . . are discursively constructed.' (4.22)

'the "real world" is created by language.' (4.23)

'The linguistic habits within a culture create what becomes the "real world".' (4.23)

The portentousness of such theoretical assertions invites a first response of, 'Wow!' or 'Gee!' or 'You don't say!' In short, we are impressed. It certainly sounds as if something important is being said or, that, at the very least, the student authors think they are saying something important and original.

The vagueness, however, emerges as soon as we enquire about what—precisely—this 'something' is. And when we seek an answer to this question through a close examination of the empirical examples students provide to support or validate the generalisations, it pretty soon emerges that what is true in them is not original and what is original is not true. That is, to say that human beings give meaning to everything they see, hear, touch, use and experience, and that they do this predominantly through the language they use, is hardly an original insight.[1] Nor does it follow from this that they can change or alter everything they see, hear, touch, use and experience just by changing the language they use in regard to it. They clearly cannot do this in regard to a wide range of material substances and constraints that enter even into forms of reality we might call 'social' (because human action and interaction also enters into them). Moreover, although there may, at any given time, be socially and politically dominant ways of describing and explaining the social world, or some aspect of it, in language, these ways very often (always?) coexist with alternative ways even in the same human society at the same time. In addition, even socially dominant forms of understanding change over time, quickly or slowly, depending on the empirical example or case. This means it cannot be true, in any universal, generalisable or unproblematic sense, that reality is socially constructed if this means 'constructed in only one way'; still less so if it means 'constructed in only one way all the time'. Thus, where the proposition reality is socially constructed is determinist (i.e., means 'is constructed in one and only one way') it is nearly always false. And where it is *not* determinist (i.e., means 'is constructed in a variety of ways by a variety of people for a variety of purposes') it is true, but both unoriginal and, largely, vacuous.

The social construction of reality

The most fascinating aspect of all but one of the theses is that they begin by embracing general or rhetorical forms of 'social constructivism' that certainly *sound* strongly unitary and determinist, but they almost always end up endorsing—in fact, if not in theory—a variety that is much more cautiously and conventionally pluralist. However, the authors generally do this despite themselves, as it were, through a species of self-contradiction. They write theses of the form 'language constructs the social world in *this* way (singular) but I see through this construction and reject it'. But, of course, if they can see through the construction and reject it, why (one might ask) can others not do so too? And if others *do* do so, then in what sense is the construction socially or politically dominant? Or, rather, whatever one might choose to say about that dominance it is clear that it does *not* equate to unchallenged monopoly.

One of the theses quoted at length in Appendix 5 (POLS/ IR 18) is rather more subtle than this, in that its author explicitly acknowledges the variety of discourses (dominant and oppositional) at play in Australian political debates about asylum seekers. But this acknowledgement only leads the student in question into deeper philosophical confusion. S/he quite clearly sees that none of the discourses in question are clearly and unambiguously false (i.e., involves denying or lying about known facts)[2] and therefore thinks that to deal with them s/he has to put the issue of truth in philosophical brackets, and deal exclusively with what is 'regarded as true' in political debate.

In fact, such bracketing is unnecessary. Once one has clearly grasped that human descriptions of the world are not simple 'copies' or 'reflections' of reality, but accounts actively constructed for specific purposes, then it is not extraordinary, but rather quite common, to find that there can be a variety of true descriptions of the same reality—each of which emphasises different aspects or features of that reality.

Debates over these descriptions then become, in effect, debates over which aspects or features of reality one should foreground and background, and such debates are very often also—simultaneously—debates about the different political values and ethical beliefs that describers are expressing through, and embodying in, those descriptions. So, to take the student's own example (5.14–5.16), some people seeing 'boat people' as queue jumpers, threats to Australia's borders and as a security and diplomatic problem, and other people seeing them as[3] persecuted human beings and refugees obliging Australia 'to fulfil the ancient and universal virtue' of 'taking in a stranger in need' is just one instance of a humanly commonplace kind of debate about how a reality should properly or appropriately be described.[4] It need raise no issues of philosophical relativism, and no deep questions about the nature of truth.

As I observe in my comments, the only reason the author of POLS/IR 18 thinks it might or could raise such issues is that s/he is—ironically—operating a classically *Tractatus* conception of description (as reflection or copying) while supposedly basing his/her thesis on a postmodernist critique of such conceptions.

This shows, I think, just how deep *Tractatus*-type assumptions about knowledge and reality run in academia (even in radical academia), and I try to explain why this is so in Chapter 7.

The social construction of subjectivity

With the exception of the author of POLS/IR 18 however, the rest of the student authors operate the self-contradiction of problematising social constructions while alleging them to be dominant entirely unselfconsciously. This becomes particularly ironic when students are dealing with 'the social construction of subjectivity'. They are continually found saying that identities (including gender and ethnic identities) are socially constructed but that their understanding of identity (whether that of others or their own) is not—or that, if it is, it is socially constructed in ways that run diametrically counter to the dominant ones.

This immediately raises the issue of the supposed power of dominance again. In the case of gender and sex in particular it also involves students sailing extremely close to the wind of a flat-out philosophical idealism, where human beings can, apparently, be any sex that they want to be. Again, it is important to see precisely what is wrong with this. It is not that one cannot enact one's sex performatively if one wishes, irrespective of one's biology (5.17 and 5.23–24). One can. But there will be biological limits on that performance if one has, say, breasts that do not lactate, or a vagina but no womb. Also, in a broader context, if such performance involves, for example, 'men' who never impregnate women, or 'women' who never get impregnated or cannot be impregnated, some long-term issues of species survival will eventually arise. Or rather they would, unless you think (as I do) that Darwin was right and that species survival is not the kind of thing that depends on performative 'preference' (of at least the vast majority of the members of any living species).

5. Language and discourse

I hope it is now obvious to the reader that most of the student authors straightforwardly equate discourse with language. Where this happens, it often goes along with a strong linguistic determinism in which, at least in their opening theoretical salvos, something called language has 'incredible power' to do this or that, or cause this or that, or (more frequently) determine this or that. In the theses where language and discourse become synonymous, discourse is also predicated with similar power to 'construct' this, that or the other linguistically. Passages embodying this kind of determinism have been quoted repeatedly in earlier chapters so I will not offer further examples here.

However, a minority of the student theses in my sample commence with a rather more sophisticated approach in which, in their opening theoretical protocols at least, discourse and language are firmly distinguished. The authors make it clear that discourse involves practices other than speaking, writing or reading. The general trend of this kind of analysis is to suggest that all human practices, and indeed all products of such practices, have meaning, so that the power of discourse is not simply the power of language, but the power of a whole set of linguistic and non-linguistic practices to create both the world and the subjectivities of the subjects acting in that world.

Despite this apparent greater theoretical sophistication, however, it is significant that when these student authors start deploying their theoretical apparatus empirically, they almost without exception fall back into equating discourse with language (6.1–6.5). More than that, just like their less-sophisticated colleagues, they tend to deploy both discourse and language as single theoretical *subjects* capable of doing or determining this or that, etc. (2.3/6.2 and 2.4/6.5).

One of the main reasons why this happens is that, while the more theoretically sophisticated authors may begin by talking generally—and in the abstract—about practices other than the use of language (6.4), this is almost invariably as far as they go. Once the substantive analysis commences, no other examples of meaning-laden practices beyond language use even get a mention so that, by default as it were, discourse reduces to language again.

Furthermore, the treatment of language, even by this more-sophisticated minority of authors is conceptually exceedingly narrow. That is the use of language, even in these theses, is equated with the meaning of words. No reference is made to (for example) tone of voice, facial expression or bodily movements accompanying speech.

Interestingly, however, one thesis—which is concerned with dance as a meaning-laden practice—does have to concern itself in a more nuanced way with the difference between language and dance, with the latter being explicitly conceptualised as a form of non-linguistic discourse (6.6–6.11). However, even in this case, the student author eventually falls back into a focus on the *limitations* of dance as a form of discourse in comparison with language. S/he sees these limitations as especially acute because s/he equates language purely with the meaning of words. S/he does not even consider the bodily accompaniments of speech or gesture alternatives to speech, both of which can bring the use of language closer to dance as a meaning-conferring practice than s/he allows. Significantly, too, even this author tends to conceive language as a unitary subject able to do this or that (6.11).

The next chapter considers in more philosophical depth why all the authors writing in the poststructuralist or postmodernist theoretical tradition find it difficult—indeed almost impossible— to sustain the language/discourse distinction even when they begin by making it and insisting upon it conceptually. I will suggest that the underlying reason is to be found in the dominating theoretical metaphor they are using—that of a landscape, space or world observed from outside. I will also suggest that this metaphor tends to affect theorists' conceptions of language and of the use of language in ways that are profoundly distorting and almost bound to lead—often despite initial disclaimers—to deterministic formulations in which subjects appear as the hapless prisoners of language or discourse. For the moment, however, I simply want to demonstrate that the theoretical difficulty students have in maintaining the language/discourse distinction is both profound and real, as will be apparent from the quotations in Appendix 6 and my comments upon them.

PART II

loosening the coils:
Wittgenstein

6. An outsider's view of the world: The contemplative stance of the theorist

This chapter is the first in the book not to be based on an analysis of quotations from student theses. This is because its central focus is on what students do not say, on what they do not even notice let alone reflect upon, even in the most deeply theoretical parts of their theses.

When Wittgenstein discusses talk about 'mental processes and states and . . . behaviourism' in his *Philosophical Investigations*, he says, *inter alia*,

> The first step is the one that altogether escapes notice. We talk of processes and states and leave their nature undecided. Sometime we shall know more about them—we think. But that is just what commits us to a particular way of looking at the matter. For we have a definite concept of what it means to know a process better. *(The decisive movement in the conjuring trick has been made, and it was the very one that we thought most innocent).*
> PI, 308 [Emphasis added]

In this chapter I shall also be concerned with a 'first step . . . that altogether escapes notice' and is the 'decisive movement in a conjuring trick' made by student theorists. This step is one which they think 'most innocent', but which also commits them to 'a particular way of looking at the matter'. In this case, however, the matter is not mental processes and states, but human society and the entities (things) that compose it.

The crucial starting point is an observation I made in Chapter 1 when discussing the set of metaphors that students learn to deploy when doing poststructural or postmodern theory:

> It will readily be apparent that in all the quotations in Appendix 1, in fact in virtually all the quotations in all the appendices, first-person pronouns and forms of the verb are entirely absent. In short, there are no 'I think's, 'I feel's, 'It seems to me's, etc., let alone any openly introspective or reflexive passages. This form of theoretical prose is, in short, rigidly objectivist both in the sense that it conjures up a world of objects affected or moved only by mechanical or inanimate forces, but also in the sense that the prose itself appears to have no subject or creator. It is an object produced by some kind of 'automatic' or 'mechanical' process (precisely the process of 'theorising'). We shall investigate the deep significance of this latter point in Chapter 6.

It is now time for us to investigate the 'deep significance' of this matter. To do so we have to change imaginings. Let us suppose that, instead of standing imaginatively outside society to theorise about it, the student theorist were to place him or herself *in* the social world, space or landscape, and to invoke 'theoretically' what they do *in* that world and how they describe what they see *in* that landscape.

A simple logical preparation for this type of theorising is for the student authors to change a crucial part of speech: to replace third-person forms of the subject and verb with first-person forms. For example, not *subjects use language* or *subjects are socially constructed*, but 'I say', or 'I think' or 'I say to them' and 'they say to me in reply'.

Making such a shift in form of speech simultaneously creates a shift in observational perspective. The observer is no longer imaginatively suspended somewhere (and 'Where?' is a good question)[1] 'outside' or 'above' society, looking down, as it were, on masses of anonymous subjects and subjectivities. Now s/he is imaginatively 'at the same level' or 'in the same space' as everybody else—'looking them in the eye' as it were, and having to address them, and to listen to their replies, on equal terms.

And something else happens when the observer makes this shift of imaginative perspective, and in its accompanying forms of speech. Once s/he is in society, s/he can no longer see language or discourse as an abstract object. Rather, s/he becomes a person *in* society talking, writing, reading and saying, *in* these various forms of language, what s/he wants to say. Moreover, from this changed perspective it is extraordinarily hard, if not impossible, to see language or discourse as any kind of abstract subject/object that does or constructs anything, or has any kind of power.

Of course, those of us who are at all reflective will realise that we did not personally, individually, create the language(s) we use *ab initio* as it were. Rather, we learn a 'pre-given' language or languages, grow up speaking it or them, and are therefore committed to the meanings that language carries long before we reflect upon or question those meanings (if, indeed, we ever do).

The question now is, does this fact in any way tightly determine what I may say or think in this world, or what you may say or think in this world, or what they may say or think in this world? Does it, for example, preclude or make impossible certain ways of thinking—for me, or you, or them?

One great philosopher thinks not, and gives good reasons why.

It need not be so. For I can give the concept 'number' rigid limits in this way, that is, use the word number for a rigidly limited concept, but I can also use it so the extension of the concept is *not* closed by a frontier. And this is how we do use the word 'game'. For how is the concept of a game bounded? What still counts as a game and what no longer does? Can you give the boundary? No. You can *draw* one; for none has so far been drawn. (But that never troubled you before when you used the word 'game'.) *PI*, 68

But if the concept 'game' is uncircumscribed like that, you don't really know what you mean by a 'game'—When I give the description: 'The ground was quite covered with plants' do you want to say I don't know what I am talking about until I can give the definition of a plant? *PI*, 70

One might say that the concept 'game' is a concept with blurred edges.—But is a blurred concept a concept at all?—Is an indistinct photograph a picture of a person at all? Is it even always an advantage to replace an indistinct picture by a sharp one? Isn't an indistinct one often exactly what we need?

Frege compares a concept to an area and says that an area with vague boundaries cannot be called an area at all. This presumably means that we cannot do anything with it.—But is it senseless to say 'Stand roughly there?' Suppose that I were standing with someone in a city square and said that. As I say it I do not draw any kind of boundary, but perhaps point with my hand—as if I were indicating a particular spot. And this is how one might explain to someone what a game is. One gives examples and intends them to be taken in a particular way.—I do not however mean by this that he is supposed to see in those examples that common thing which I—for some reason—was unable to express; but that he is now to *employ* those examples in a particular way. Here giving examples is not an indirect means of explaining—in default of a better. For any general definition can be misunderstood too. The point is *this* is how we play the game. (I mean the language-game with the word 'game'.) *PI,* 71

If I tell someone 'Stand roughly there'—may not this explanation work perfectly? And cannot every other one fail too?

But isn't it an inexact explanation? Yes; why shouldn't we call it inexact? Only let us understand what 'inexact' means. For it does not mean 'unusable'. And let us consider what we call an 'exact' explanation in contrast with this one. Perhaps something like drawing a chalk line around an area. Here it strikes us at once that the line has breadth. So a colour-edge would be more exact. *But has this exactness still got a function here: isn't the engine idling? PI,* 88 [Emphasis added]

But when one draws a boundary it may be for various kinds of reason. If I surround an area with a fence or a line or otherwise, the purpose may be to prevent someone from getting in or out; but it may be part of a game and the players may be supposed, say, to jump over the boundary; or it may show where the property of one man ends and that of another begins; and so on. *So if I draw a boundary line that is not yet to say what I am drawing it for. PI,* 499 [Emphasis added]

I can think of no better expression to characterise these similarities than 'family resemblances'; for the various resemblances between members of a family: build, features, colour of eyes, gait, temperament etc. etc. overlap and criss-cross in the same way.—and I shall say 'games' form a family.

And for instance the kinds of number form a family in the same way. Why do we call something a 'number'? Well, perhaps because it has a—direct—relationship with several things that have hitherto been called number; and this can be said to give it an indirect relationship to other things we call the same name. *And we extend our concept of number as in spinning a thread we twist fibre on fibre.* *PI,* 67 [Emphasis added]

Look at the sentence as an instrument, and its sense as its employment. *PI,* 421

Language is an instrument. Its concepts are instruments . . . *PI,* 569

But how many kinds of sentences are there? . . . There are *countless* kinds: countless different kinds of uses of what we call 'symbols', 'words', 'sentences'. And this multiplicity is not something fixed, given once and for all; *but new types of language, new language-games, as we may say, come into existence, and others become obsolete and get forgotten* . . . Hence the term language-game is meant to bring into prominence the fact that the *speaking* of a language is part of an *activity*, or of a form of life. *PI,* 23 [Emphasis added]

What we call '*descriptions*' are instruments for particular uses. Think of a machine-drawing, a cross-section, an elevation with measurements, which an engineer has before him. Thinking of a description as a word-picture of the facts has something misleading about it: one tends to think only of such pictures as hang on our walls: which seem simply to portray how a thing looks, what it is like. (*These pictures are as it were idle.*) *PI,* 291 [Emphasis added]

Must I not rather ask, 'What does the description do anyway? What purpose does it serve?' In another context, indeed, we know what is a complete and incomplete description. Ask yourself: How do we use the expressions 'complete' or 'incomplete description'? Giving a complete (or incomplete) report of a speech. Is it part of this to report the tone of voice, the play of expression, the genuineness or falsity of feeling, the intentions of the speaker, the strain of speaking*? Whether this or that belongs to a complete description will depend on the purpose of the description,* on what the recipient does with the description. *Zettel,* 311[2] [Emphasis added]

It does not take much acuity, I think, to see that Wittgenstein is presenting a completely different view of language to that which predominates in the student theses. And this formulation is right in both the literal and figurative sense of 'view'. That is, Wittgenstein is both presenting a very different and much less deterministic *conception* of language than the ones examined earlier (in that sense, 'a different view'). But he is also looking at language from a different view*point*—looking at it, we may say, 'from inside' as a user, rather than 'from above' as an analyst or theorist. Indeed, as we shall see, Wittgenstein does not think that one *can* look at language 'as a whole' or 'from the outside'—to try to do so is akin to trying to look at the universe 'as a whole' or 'from the outside'. But we will come to that later.

For the moment I want to concentrate on the close connection between these two senses of Wittgenstein's 'view' of language. That is, Wittgenstein has a much less deterministic conception of language *because* he is looking at it 'from the inside' or 'as a user'. From his position *in* the landscape, *in* society, he is asking how 'we' use this or that word ('number' or 'game' for example); whether all the concepts 'we' use are 'closed with a boundary' or need to be; what it is 'we' do when we explain things or describe things with words; or how many kinds of sentences there are for 'us' to use. And the general trend of his answers to these questions is markedly non-deterministic.

Wittgenstein stresses, for example, that concepts can be closed by a definitional boundary, which we give 'for a certain purpose', but they do not have to be closed to be usable in many contexts. More to the point, if they are so closed, they cannot be 'extended' into new uses. But language grows and develops as human society grows and develops, precisely through this process of extending concepts from one use to another. So, for example, the concept of a number can be 'extended' from counting whole objects to counting parts of objects (decimals and fractions); or from counting groups or collections of objects (cardinal numbers) to counting sequences of objects or of events (ordinal numbers).

Wittgenstein also stresses that it is a mistake to suppose that the meanings of words always have to be exact, or that words are unusable if their meanings are inexact. Indeed, he shows by one example after another (only a few of which I have presented here) that it makes no sense to call any word or concept 'exact' or 'inexact' in abstraction from the purpose for which it is being employed. Thus the accuracy of the statement, 'Look at the hillside, it's covered in beautiful flowers!' is in no way compromised because its speaker (a young man out for a walk with his girlfriend) does not know the botanical names of all the flowers involved, and only has the vaguest notion of how photosynthesis works. But, of course, a scientific botanical survey of the hillside *would* require descriptions of the flowers well beyond 'flowers' or 'beautiful'.

What is true of individual words is true of the complex sequences of words we call 'descriptions' or 'explanations'. Whether a description or explanation is 'exact' or 'vague', 'complete' or 'incomplete', 'acceptable' or 'defective' depends on the purpose for which that description or explanation is being created and given, not on some set of formal characteristics of the description or explanation itself. (For example, its concepts being tightly defined, or the logical relations between all its terms being formally specified.)

The fact that descriptions are, as Wittgenstein says, 'instruments for particular purposes' also has the important implication, referred to earlier, that there can be a variety of true descriptions of the same reality. To extend the argument from one of the quotations above, no one looking at the plan of a house renovation would say that a 'cross-section' drawing of it was true, while the 'elevation with measurements' was false.[3] But we are apt to forget this rather important fact when it comes (for example) to debating whether a serial child molester 'is' an 'evil maniac' or 'a sad case of a deep-seated personality disorder'; or whether asylum seekers 'are' 'threats to our security' or 'suffering humanity requiring our help'. In the former case we see 'clearly' and 'obviously' that *both* projections can be 'accurate' or 'true'; however we may think that in the latter cases one or other description *must* be false, as they seem so obviously 'contrasting' or 'opposed'.

But, and to repeat, this does not have to be the case if both descriptions are presented, and argumentatively supported, in ways that do not contradict known facts either about the child molester or the boat people. However, if they do contradict such facts, one or other or, indeed, both descriptions can be found false or partially false.

This latter point is especially important because, as we shall see in Chapter 10, some of the student theses advocate forms of philosophical relativism in which descriptive statements and propositions can be 'true', even though they contradict known facts, because what truth is, and what facts are, is itself a socially or culturally varied matter. I reject entirely such forms of relativism, as Wittgenstein would have, despite the quotations above emphasising the range of possible true descriptions. Such a range exists, but false descriptions always fall outside it.

To continue with Wittgensteinian exegesis for the moment—I think that both these ideas—the purposive 'extension' or 'projection' of concepts into new uses, and the purpose-dependent conception of the meaning of sentences and propositions—have profound implications for most of the sociological and political matters with which the student theses are concerned.

They imply, for example, that:

■ how an object in the world is conceptualised or classified depends as much on the uses that human beings make of it, as on any of its physical characteristics. (I may say 'Have a seat!' and point someone to a sawn-off tree stump.); and

■ how a particular part of language *itself* is classified depends on the uses speakers are making of it. Thus whether a sentence counts as a description, or an explanation, or something else entirely, depends on the way it is employed or used, not on the words in it. ('I've been for my lunch' can be a description, an explanation, a joke, an excuse, or a celebration—the opening of a new café, for example—depending on the context in which, and thus the purpose for which, it is employed.)

If all this is true for supposedly 'simple' objects such as tree stumps or flowers, or supposedly 'simple' concepts such as 'number' or 'game', how much more is it likely to be true for 'complex' concepts of the social and political world or for propositions about that world? Thus a 'parliament' or 'legislature' can be a group of well-off people meeting in a billion-dollar building in Canberra or Washington, but it can also be a group of African tribal elders meeting beneath a baobab tree, or a group of English Roundheads meeting in a field. And what is true of 'parliament' or 'legislature' is true of 'voting' or 'protesting' or of what we may mean when we speak of a political 'party' or 'faction' or 'caucus'. Think, too, of all the different things we *might* mean by saying that someone is 'rich' or 'poor' or 'powerful' or 'powerless'; or what a range of things might be meant by saying that she 'has a job' or is 'unemployed' or is 'a student', or that she is a 'racist' or 'opposes racism'.

But perhaps the most politically and socially significant aspects of Wittgenstein's insights emerge when we put together the very varied purposes we may have for 'drawing boundaries' around concepts, and the uses of concepts in propositions and sentences.

Think, for example, of saying, 'Of course, all Australians are equal as voters. My vote is fully the equal of James Packer's.' Depending on the purpose for which I say this, I might be denying that economic riches are influential in the political process, or at least trying to qualify 'radical' assertions that they are. I might, however, be being ironic. By invoking the name of James Packer, I am inviting you, as Wittgenstein says, to 'jump over' the boundary I have drawn around the concept of 'the equality of voters'. In fact, if I am being ironic, then I have drawn the boundary in order to have it challenged, to invite you to question the reality of the 'equality' I have just defined. That is, sometimes we define— draw boundaries around—words not in order to clarify or fix their meaning, but as part of a variety of *actions*: to provoke disagreement, to persuade others through irony, to make others aware of some form or other of self-contradiction, or even to draw attention to one's own dishonesties. ('If being a non-sexist male is, among other things, to take a fair share of housework, then I have to face the fact that . . .')

I could go on. But when I, and Wittgenstein, have said all this, what precisely remains of the notion of language or discourse as a kind of prison that determines what its users can think, feel or do? Surely the very notion that language is such a prison, or such a determining force, comes from looking at it in a certain kind of way? In fact, we can be more precise than that. For language to be any *thing*—a force, a prison, even a determining context—we have first to conceive 'it' as an 'it', as some kind of unity, entity or thing. As Wittgenstein also points out, the only reason, at bottom, that we think of language as a unity is that it is made up entirely of words.[4]

But the whole thrust of his later philosophy is to show that, while all words are words, and all words have meaning, how they get and change that meaning (i.e., the myriad ways in which they are used or employed) is as varied and different as any conception of variation and difference we can imagine.

Wittgenstein himself often analogises words, sentences and propositions to 'tools' or 'instruments' that we can use for a variety of purposes. He does so to emphasise that:

- ■ words are as varied a collection of types or sorts of tools as we might find in the most capacious tool box or tool shed. Therefore saying that 'they are all tools' (saying that 'they are all words') does not tell one anything of much interest about them. More importantly,

- ■ the extent of variation in the tools' use is not set by their physical properties, but precisely by the *uses* people make of them. Thus, you can use a hammer to knock in a nail, but you can also use it to pull out a nail, prise open a lock, prop a door back, dig a hole in the ground, or attack someone.

Quotes from Wittgenstein

'Think of the tools in a tool-box: there is a hammer, pliers, a saw, a screw-driver, a rule, a glue-pot, nails and screws.—The functions of words are as diverse as the functions of these objects. (And in both cases there are similarities.)

Of course what confuses us is the uniform appearance of words when we hear them spoken or meet them in script and print. For their *application* is not presented to us so clearly. Especially when we are doing philosophy!' [And social theory!]. *PI*, 11

'When we say: "Every word in language signifies something" we have so far said *nothing whatsoever*; unless we have explained exactly what distinction we wish to make . . .

'Imagine someone's saying, "*All* tools serve to modify something. Thus the hammer modifies the position of the nail, the saw the shape of the board, and so on"—And what is modified by the rule, the glue-pot, the nails?— "Our knowledge of a thing's length, the temperature of the glue, and the solidity of the box."—Would anything be gained by this assimilation of expressions?' *PI*, 13 and 14 [emphases in original]

[Social theory is actually *full* of this kind of empty 'assimilation of (linguistic) expressions' masquerading as universalist 'theoretical' insight. Thus, as well as 'every word—or sign—signifies something' we have 'all individuals play social roles', 'all states pursue power', 'all identities are socially constructed', etc.]

And so it is with words and sentences. Ultimately their meanings are as various as *the purposes* for which human beings use or employ them. So, if we analogise the dictionary definitions of individual words to the physical shapes and properties of various tools, then just as tools can be put to various uses, some of them completely unintended by those who designed or created them, so words can be put to various uses, uses which may involve extending, or even significantly altering, their dictionary definitions. Thus a tree can perfectly properly be defined as a kind of plant, but a family tree is not any kind of plant.

The human purposes that determine the uses to which words and combinations of words are put, are not only various, they are often also contradictory or conflicting. We use words to disagree with each other, even to fight with each other, and sometimes those disagreements or fights will be over the words themselves. (For example, the meaning of 'freedom', or 'truth', 'sovereignty', 'equality' or 'justice', the meaning of 'being sane' or 'being normal', etc.)

The point is, however, that our language allows us to have *whatever* agreements we want, *whatever* disagreements we want, *whatever* preferences we have, *whatever* enthusiasms, revulsions, exultations, criticisms, jealousies, generosities, meannesses we manifest. This is not to say that language has no limits, but that its limits are only the limits of the purposes that we human beings can have at any given place, in any given time.

As we change those purposes—as what we imagine, desire or wish to do changes—so we either find new words to accommodate these changes or (more frequently) we use old words in new ways to facilitate and encourage new purposes, actions and interactions. As Wittgenstein stresses, *no* word is definitively, and for all time, 'closed with a boundary', so *all* words are available for new uses—for extensions or projections of their existing meanings. Of course, that all words are so available does not mean that they will be so used. There may be nobody who wishes to use them in new ways. Or there may be some who do, but who lose out in power struggles with those who wish to maintain old meanings. (Current examples include the struggles in some societies over the traditional and extended meanings of 'marriage' and 'family'.)

The point is, however, that whether or not the meanings of words or sentences are 'extended' or 'projected', whether or not new uses are made of them for new purposes, has nothing to do with the words themselves—with language 'itself'. Rather, it depends on the people who use words. Power is certainly a factor, but it is not the power of 'words' or 'discourse', it is the power (or powerlessness) of people—including the differential power to change words or resist their change. And isn't that 'obvious' conclusion just what we should expect to find now that we have unravelled this particular knot in our thinking?

One final point. It is true that, at any given time, in any given society, there will be dominant interpretations of the meaning of words (words such as 'sex', 'family' and 'justice', or 'normal' or 'natural' behaviour). In so far as these dominant, standard or normal meanings and interpretations are endlessly repeated and reiterated, and seem to be accepted by most people, it is easy to think of them as having some power over the minds and actions of those who use and accept them.

As I have said previously, however, in nearly all cases where there are dominant interpretations, there are also 'counter' or 'alternative' interpretations at play (whose presence is signalled by, among other things, continual complaints about dominant interpretations!). And since, by definition, those who offer such counter interpretations are not in the power of the allegedly dominant ones, it seems to me that the appropriate way to describe this contradictory state of affairs is to say that the people who accept the dominant interpretations are 'insufficiently reflective', rather than that they are 'in the power of language' or 'constructed by discourse'. Or, to be precise, they may be in the power of language or constructed by discourse but only because they are insufficiently reflective people.

Of course, to put things in such a way implies that the conventional majority are dumb offenders rather than hapless victims and might make linguistic and political radicals even more unpopular than they already are ('Fucking elitists!'). Telling the truth doesn't win popularity contests. Anyway, the dominant majority may not be dumb, or offending. They may, in fact, be just as reflective as the radicals but have come to different—i.e., socially orthodox—conclusions on the basis of those reflections. This, however, is a question that requires empirical research into majority and minority views and their claimed justifications, rather than some arrogant assumption of a linguistically induced 'majority' blindness that (of course) one does not share.

7. Theory and *Tractatus* epistemology

> An earthquake only has meaning, we only 'know' an earthquake because we also know things that are part earthquake (an earth tremor) or not earthquake (a relatively stable geological formation). There *is* no 'reality' accessible to us outside thought; an object has existence, but not one meaning which constitutes its reality. What gives an object reality is our thought, our 'knowing' of it. We endow 'reality' through 'naming' and we cannot name or know in this sense, outside of a discursive structure. (4.21/6.5)

The above is an unusually blunt and direct statement of the epistemological view which dominates, to one degree or another, all the theses reviewed in this book. I say, 'to one degree or another' because, while all those who are committed to any notion of the 'social construction of reality' must deny that 'there is [any] reality accessible to us outside thought', very few of the student authors go on to elaborate this view in the explicitly philosophical way found above.

What is most interesting, however, is the way in which this elaboration occurs. As the quotation shows, these explicitly philosophical remarks occur in the context of a discussion of 'an earthquake'. In this discussion:

- an earthquake is treated as an 'object'.
- it is given as an example of 'an object' which we 'know' because the student thinks, or at any rate appears to think, that all knowledge is knowledge of 'objects'. It follows
- that the way we know objects is by perceiving or observing them; then
- when we perceive or observe them and give them a name, we simultaneously give them meaning. Hence
- objects (apparently) 'exist', whether we know them or not, but they do not become *real* until we know them/name them.

I outline the manifold, and basic, philosophical confusions found in this passage in my discussion of it in Appendix 4, so I will not repeat those comments here. What I will do, however, is elaborate on the remark I made in the course of those comments—'The assertion that "we endow 'reality'" through "naming" is pure *Tractatus* epistemology.'

The *Tractatus Logico-Philosophicus*, first published in German in 1921, was the young Wittgenstein's first great work of philosophy, and in fact his only book of philosophy published during his lifetime. Wittgenstein gradually became dissatisfied with the ideas he had expressed in that book. After his return from Austria to Cambridge in 1929 he began to make more and more critical revisions of these ideas, revisions which, by the time he wrote the manuscript that became Part I of the *Philosophical Investigations* (in the late 1930s and early 1940s), had become tantamount to a total rejection.

This is very significant for our current purposes, because the following ideas had been central to the *Tractatus*.

1. The world is made up of objects.
2. Individual words in language name objects.

3. By arranging these 'naming' words in *propositions* (i.e., in sentences or statements that assert 'what is the case') human beings make knowledge or 'truth claims' about the world.

4. Some truth claims are true, i.e., assert the existence of states of affairs that are real. Others are false, i.e., assert the existence of states of affairs that, though logically possible, turn out not to be real.

5. *All* forms of language that are *not* propositional—that do *not* assert the existence of factual states of affairs (and are therefore not testable as true or false)—are 'meaningless' or 'nonsense'.

It is not appropriate or necessary to trace in detail here the complex intellectual history of Wittgenstein's increasing—and in the end total—rejection of his *Tractatus* philosophy. It is enough to say that by the end of this process Wittgenstein had concluded that it was the very conception of the problem he had been addressing in the book—i.e., the problem of the relationship of language to the world—that had led him most profoundly astray. In the *Philosophical Investigations* this conception is held to have been defective, not in one way, but in a number of intellectually deep, and deeply related, ways, such as:

■ that conceptualising 'language' and 'the world' as two separate 'things' (and then asking about their 'relations') had made it impossible for him, for example, to conceive language as a thing *in* the world, rather than as a separate means of 'naming' the world. Further,

■ the words 'language' and 'the world' are words that treat as a unity—as one 'thing' or 'things'—enormously complex collections of very disparate phenomena. In particular,

■ 'language' is not a single thing in any sense other than it consists entirely of words, and this common feature masks much more important differences in the *use* of words. But,

■ to speak of the *use* of words is to speak of the *users* of words—of *people*—and people, purposefully acting creatures, had been entirely absent in the *Tractatus*. That is, they appeared neither as users of language nor as part of 'the world'. However,

■ once people as active users of language are introduced into the problem, then 'the problem' as originally conceived ('the relationship of language to the world') disappears, or is entirely recast. Because,

■ now language does not have to be related to the world, because people relate language to the world by using language in the world. Hence,

■ if we really want to understand, not language, but the *use* of language, then we need not logic, but an understanding of the multifarious purposes for which people use language. That is to say,

■ we must understand speaking, writing and reading as purposeful activities in the world, and as part of, or accompaniments to, other activities. And further

■ it is far easier to do this—to conceive the use of language as an activity and as part of other activities— by looking at both language and the world from a first-person point of view (the point of view of the *Philosophical Investigations*) rather than from a third-person, contemplative or observatory point of view, one supposedly outside or above both language and the world (the *Tractatus* point of view).

Now I think all this makes some things fairly clear. First, despite their supposed poststructuralist or postmodernist novelty and sophistication, all our student authors are in fact stuck in an epistemology that was seriously problematised and (in my view) effectively discredited some 70 years ago! Second, it is only fair to note that this is in no way surprising, as large areas of the academic social sciences, up to and including their 'radical' fringes, are still stuck in this epistemology. So in this respect the students are simply reproducing what they are dominantly taught as 'theory', by both teachers who are sympathetic to poststructuralist approaches and those who are not.

The question of why this God-like, contemplative or obser-vational epistemological stance on the world (including the social world) has such a tenacious hold in academia, despite having been radically undermined first by Wittgenstein, then by several succeeding generations of 'ordinary language' philosophers, is an interesting one, on which I have speculated at length elsewhere.[1] Suffice it to say here that, at least for Wittgenstein, part of the answer is that the very multiplicity, complexity and variety of ways in which people use language *itself* make it very difficult for them to have a 'clear view' or understanding of how they are using it. Therefore, in place of that clear view, which is very hard to attain, people (both professional intellectuals and ordinary language users) substitute an *a priori* theory that language is a naming or labelling device—a sort of transparent cloak with words written on it that we 'throw over' the world to give it meaning—a theory that is not so much false as radically partial and (therefore) misleading.

For our purposes, the most important implication of the *Philosophical Investigations* critique of the *Tractatus* episte-mology—especially the crucial change of view from a third- to a first-person conception of language and the world that it entails—concerns the 'social construction of reality', the idea that language or discourse constructs the world—and that is central to *all* the student theses surveyed in this book.

To grasp that crucial implication we need only to consider any simple 'descriptive' use of language. Suppose I am in a room with another person who gets up from his chair and walks across the room to a light switch near the door and then switches the light on. If, as Wittgenstein says, 'I am doing philosophy', it will instantly strike me that I cannot describe or report even this very simple, homely act, performed directly in front of me, except by means of language or some other descriptive 'signifier' (say a video of the act, or a drawing or photograph of my friend walking across the room). And the way this is often put is to say that the act can 'occur' but it cannot be 'known' except through some 'system of signification'. And then, since we are doing philosophy we generalise. If such a simple act, and its material setting (the room, the door, the light switch) cannot be known except through language, then clearly nothing can be known except through language, and (therefore) there is no reality that is not linguistic reality. (Or, rather, there is no reality that is not 'signified' reality, and language is the most commonly used signifier).

But now, suppose I conceive a situation in which the person who is to walk across the room and turn the light on is me myself. Instead of actually walking across the room and turning the light on, however, I sit in my chair and I say (repeatedly), 'I am walking across the room and putting the light on.' And while I am sitting there and saying this sentence, I am also writing it out repeatedly with pen and paper. I draw a picture of myself walking across the room to accompany the words. I then type the sentence into my notebook computer, over 150 times. Then I get out my mobile phone, phone my closest friend, and say, 'Hey Bob, I am walking across the room and putting the light on.' Now if, when I have finished all this linguistic and representational activity—all this signifying and describing—I am still sitting there in my chair, will I have walked across the room and put the light on?

Even to ask the question is almost insulting, so obvious is the answer 'No', or 'No, of course not!' But that answer is only so obvious because the first-person perspective I adopted in the paragraph above makes it so. For if the perspective I adopt is of me describing others (whether other people, or other things, or other situations) or of others describing others, it is not nearly so obvious that the reality of acts is not exhausted by the description of acts, or that the reality of things is not exhausted by the description of things. This is because, when looking from the third-person 'outside' as it were, the only acts occurring are acts 'perceived' and 'described'; the only things existing are the things 'perceived' and 'described'. But when looking from the first-person 'inside', acts are not acts of others, that I or others perceive or describe, but acts I perform. Things are not things that I or others perceive or describe, but things I touch, use, walk on, run into, etc.

At this point, it is worth considering the implications of this change of perspective for the quotation with which I began this chapter—that extraordinary example of an earthquake. To say of a dramatic, cataclysmic, overwhelmingly physical event such as an earthquake that:

> what gives an object reality is our thought, our 'knowing' of it. We endow 'reality' through 'naming' and we cannot name or know in this sense, outside of a discursive structure ...

you *must*, it seems to me, be perceiving the earthquake imaginatively from somewhere far removed, somewhere way 'outside' or 'above' it—perhaps, from an aircraft or helicopter. So that, from a position of safety, as it were, you see the event as an object and say, 'My God, what a massive earthquake!' (Another way to have this 'objective' view of an earthquake is to view it or, more likely, its aftermath, on television, while seated comfortably in your front room.)

For if, by contrast, I imagine myself actually being *in* an earthquake, so that concrete roof beams are falling on my head, or I am being washed away in a mud slide, I would hardly, if I survived, say (or write) that because the beam fell on me unexpectedly and from behind (so that I did not even have time to cry out, let alone 'name' it before it hit me) its 'reality' did not split my skull open.

By its very extraordinariness, the earthquake example brings out very clearly the tremendous extent to which the 'social construction of reality' relies on a very narrow form of cognitivism. That is to say, in the perspective of social constructivism, human beings only relate to the world by 'knowing' it. They do not run in it, jump in it, cuddle or fight in it, swim in it, get shot, pulverised or washed away in it—they just 'know' it, and always (it seems) from afar 'object—ively'.

To put all that pretentiously, third-person linguistic per-spectives run together epistemology (questions of knowing) and ontology (questions of being) in ways that tend to lead to the latter being absorbed by the former. First-person linguistic perspectives, however, make it much easier radically to distinguish epistemology and ontology, because they make it much more 'clear' or 'obvious' that, so far as 'I' am concerned, epistemology can *never* absorb ontology.

Of course, the social world consists of, is made up of, individual human beings, and this has the following interesting implication. From the point of view of each and every individual 'I' concerning their own being in the world it is 'obvious' that in very important respects reality is *not* 'socially constructed' or 'constructed in discourse'. ('Don't tell me "parliament is socially constructed",' I say as I puff, unfitly, up Parliament Hill to the front door.) But from the point of view of each and every individual

'I' concerning the being of others in the world, it is not at all 'obvious' that reality is not, in important respects, socially constructed or constructed in discourse. ('Hey, that parliament wouldn't *be* a parliament if it wasn't called that in language. Those people going up that hill wouldn't *be* people, or on a hill, unless we had those words to say so. Wow! Blows you away that thought!')

So how to resolve or dissolve this conundrum? Well the most obvious way (one which, as far as I can see, all human beings, including philosophers, adopt in practice) is to work on the assumption that one is not unique—indeed that one's own case is universally generalisable to all other human beings. In other words, if there is an absolute ontological difference for me between sitting in a chair and *saying* I am walking across the room and putting the light on and actually getting up and putting the light on, then there is an absolute ontological difference for everybody else between their sitting in a chair and saying . . . etc. We all take it that this is so even if, when I state the difference for somebody else, I can, precisely, only state it in 'language' or some other 'signifier'—'She says she is putting the light on but actually . . .', etc.

It may now be clear why I began this book with a chapter about the metaphors used in the theoretical sections of the students' theses. It may also now be clear why I focused on the world or landscape that was constructed through those metaphors—a rigidly impersonal world of things and forces (including some 'thing' called 'language') seen from outside, and why I have returned to this issue again and again in different chapters and contexts. This is because Wittgenstein's words are absolutely apposite here—'The decisive movement in the conjuring trick *has* been made, and it *was* the very one we thought most innocent.'

Propositions such as 'reality is socially constructed' or 'society is constructed in discourse' turn out to be precisely true 'in theory'—in the world of theory. They are made true (or at any rate highly plausible) from the very beginning by the way the 'theoretical perspective' *linguistically sets up* (a) the world about which the theorist is going to theorise—objective, over there, down there—and (b) the perspective—third-person, outsider, observational—from which s/he is going to theorise.

In the greatest of ironies, the 'truth' of social constructivism turns out to be an artefact of language use. Or, more precisely, it is an artefact of the perennial tendency of this kind of theory to make overwhelming use of one form, or area, or region of language (third-person, other-oriented, objective—even about subjectivities—and concerned with other people only in the massive unknown plural—'they', 'them') and almost *no use* at all of another form or region (first-person, self-oriented, subjective about subjectivity and concerned with small numbers of known others—'you', 'us'). Indeed theorists often ban these latter uses of language as being 'non-theoretical', 'subjective' or 'journalistic', etc. But banning these uses means that students cannot learn by using them, cannot see what can be seen much more clearly when you do use them. In fact, radical forms of social constructivism are ensuring the truth of their own perspective on the world, by banning (in the name of 'method') the very uses of language which would instantly problematise that truth.

To repeat, these 'personal' uses of language do not show that social constructivism is false. Rather, they show that this is a partial and over-simplified philosophical perspective. They show that the world (meaning by this both the physical and social world) is partially socially constructed and partially not, with the balance of those parts being crucially varied from case to case, context to context, depending on:

- what (precisely what) one is talking and writing about;
- how (precisely how) one is talking or writing about it; and

■ what else one is doing, when one is talking and writing.

Needless to say (at least, by now I hope it is needless to say) all this in turn means that language or discourse does not determine anything, although of course people may use it, in certain cases and contexts, in very deterministic ways. For let us be absolutely clear: language most certainly did not create or pre-determine the 'truth' of social constructivism. Rather it is the way the students (and the theorists they admire) *used* language that created or pre-determined the truth of social constructivism. If the students were fooled, they fooled themselves. Something called 'language' did not fool them. As we have seen, there were/are other regions, areas of language which could instantly have helped them *not* to fool themselves, but the students simply did not make use of them. Indeed they were either told, or told themselves, not to!

Addendum

The *Philosophical Investigations*, the *Tractatus Logico-Philosophicus* and 'the Augustinian picture' of language: An aside on a technical but relevant issue in Wittgensteinian exegesis

Introduction

This addendum is concerned with what may appear, at first sight, a rather technical matter in Wittgensteinian scholarship—a debate about the relationship between Wittgenstein's 'later' philosophy (the *Philosophical Investigations*) and his 'early' philosophy (the *Tractatus Logico-Philosophicus*). However, as I hope will soon become apparent, this technical debate is centrally relevant to this book, because its main focus—the so-called 'Augustinian picture of language'—is found not only in most of the honours theses discussed in this book, but in a vast range of academic writing in the social sciences, both 'radical' and conventional. Therefore, if what Wittgenstein has to say in critique of that picture is correct—and I shall try to show that it is—this has profound, indeed revolutionary implications, not only for our student authors, but for the current dominant intellectual and theoretical practices in most academic social sciences.

Wittgenstein did not arrive directly at a critique of the 'Augustinian picture'. Rather he came to it slowly, as part of his long and arduous efforts to formulate what had been wrong with his early philosophy. By the late 1930s and early 1940s (when he was writing the *Philosophical Investigations*) Wittgenstein had come to the conclusion that what was most profoundly wrong with the *Tractatus* was not anything in the book itself, but some unstated, 'commonsense' assumptions about language that had silently underlain it. The *Tractatus* was simply a formalisation and intellectualisation of those assumptions. Thus in his later philosophy it became important to him to critique, not the earlier book itself, but those unstated assumptions.

As a result, the *Tractatus* itself is mentioned very little in the *Investigations*, an omission that has led some Wittgensteinian scholars to argue that Wittgenstein's later philosophy is *not* in fact a critique of the *Tractatus* philosophy, and that the continuities between the *Tractatus* and the *Investigations* are more important or significant than the differences.[2] However, for this view even to be plausible there has to be no connection at all between 'the Augustinian picture' and the *Tractatus* philosophy, which simply is not borne out by the textual evidence. Although the *Tractatus* is mentioned explicitly only four times in the text of the *Investigations*, all those mentions are very critical in tone and, more importantly, all appear at crucial moments in the development of the *Investigations*' own argument.

Here, I want to lay out for the reader the central argumentative structure of the *Investigations* and then show how that argument is related—through 'the Augustinian picture'—both to the *Tractatus* and to the central themes of this book.

Ludwig Wittgenstein begins his *Philosophical Investigations* (hereafter '*PI*') with a passage from St Augustine's *Confessions*:

> When they (my elders) named some object, and accordingly moved toward something, I saw this and I grasped that the thing was called by the sound they uttered when they meant to point it out. Their intention was shown by their bodily movements, as it were the natural language of all peoples: the expression of the face, the play of the eyes, the movement of other parts of the body, and the tone of voice which expresses our state of mind in seeking, having, rejecting, or avoiding something. Thus, as I heard words repeatedly used in their proper places in various sentences, I gradually learnt to understand what objects they signified; and after I had trained my mouth to form these signs, I used them to express my own desires.' (*PI*, p. 2e, note 1)

Having quoted the passage Wittgenstein says:

> These words, it seems to me, give us a particular picture of the essence of human language. It is this: the individual words in language name objects—sentences are combinations of such names—In this picture of language we find the roots of the following idea: every word has a meaning. This meaning is correlated with the word. It is the object for which the word stands. *PI, 1*

And immediately, he adds:

> Augustine does not speak of there being any difference between kinds of word. If you describe the learning of

language in this way you are, I believe, thinking of nouns like 'table', 'chair', 'bread', and of people's names, and only secondarily of the names of certain actions and properties; and of the remaining kinds of word as something that will take care of itself. *PI*, 1

In short then, the central object of critique in the *PI* is not the *Tractatus Logico-Philosophicus* (hereafter '*T*'), but what is often referred to as 'the Augustinian picture of language' (hereafter 'AP') as it appears in the *Confessions*.

However this does not mean that *the T* itself escapes criticism. On the contrary, all four mentions of it in the body of the *PI* are strongly critical. In remark 23 Wittgenstein says:

It is interesting to compare the multiplicity of the tools in language and of the ways they are used, the multiplicity of kinds of word and sentence, with what logicians have said about the structure of language. (Including the author of the *Tractatus Logico-Philosophicus*.)

And remarks 46, 97 and 114, the other three explicit references to the *T*, all make the same, highly critical, point—that in his early philosophy Wittgenstein had substituted an *a priori* logical theory of how language must be, how it must work, for a concrete empirical analysis of how it does work. In remark 46 he says:

What lies behind the idea that names really signify simples—Socrates says in the *Theaetetus*: 'If I make no mistake, I have heard some people say this: there is no definition of the primary elements—so to speak—out of which we and everything else are composed; for everything that exists in its own right can only be *named*, no other determination is possible, neither that it *is* nor that it *is not* . . . But what exists in its own right has to be . . . named without any other determination. In consequence it is impossible to give an account of any primary element; for it, nothing is possible but the bare name; its name is all it has. But just as what consists of these primary elements is itself complex, so the names of the elements become descriptive language by being compounded together. For the essence of speech is the composition of names.'

Both Russell's 'individuals' and my 'objects' (*Tractatus Logico-Philosophicus*) were such primary elements. [Emphases in original]

But in critique of all this, Wittgenstein says in the immediately following remark:

But what are the simple constituent parts of which reality is composed? What are the simple constituent parts of a chair?—The bits of wood of which it is made? Or the molecules, or the atoms?—'Simple' means: not composite. And here the point is: in what sense 'composite'? It makes no sense at all to speak absolutely of the 'simple parts of a chair'…

We use the word 'composite' (and therefore the word 'simple') in an enormous number of different and differently related ways (Is the colour of a square on a chessboard simple, or does it consist of pure white and pure yellow? And is white simple, or does it consist of the colours of the rainbow? Is this length of 2 cm simple, or does it consist of two parts, each 1 cm long? But why not of one bit 3 cm long, and one bit 1 cm long measured in the opposite direction?)

To the *philosophical* question: 'Is the visual image of this tree composite, and what are its component parts?' the correct answer is: 'That depends on what you understand by "composite".' (And that is of course not an answer but a rejection of the question.) *PI*, 47

In remark 97 we have:

> Thought is surrounded by a halo.—Its essence, logic, presents an order, in fact the a priori order of the world: that is the order of *possibilities*, which must be common to both world and thought. But this order, it seems, must be *utterly simple*. It is *prior* to all experience, must run through all experience; no empirical cloudiness or uncertainty can be allowed to affect it.—It must rather be the purest crystal. But this crystal does not appear as an abstraction; but as something concrete, indeed as the most concrete, as it were the hardest thing there is (*Tractatus Logico-Philosophicus* No. 5.5563).
>
> We are under the illusion that what is peculiar, profound, essential in our investigation, resides in trying to grasp the incomparable essence of language. That is, the order existing between the concepts of proposition, word, proof, truth, experience, and so on. This order is a *super*-order existing between—so to speak *super*-concepts. Whereas of course if the words 'language', 'experience', 'world', have a use, it must be as humble a one as the words 'table', 'lamp', 'door'.

And remark 114 is the first of a crucial group of three short remarks (114–116) which essentially restate and develop the point made in 97, but in a rather more memorable form.

Thus 114 reads:

> (*Tractatus Logico-Philosophicus*, 4.5) 'The general form of propositions is: This is how things are.'—That is the kind of proposition that one repeats to oneself countless times. One thinks that one is tracing the outline of a thing's nature over and over again, and one is merely tracing round the frame through which we look at it.

Remarks 115 and 116 continue:

> A *picture* held us captive. And we could not get outside it, for it lay in our language and language seemed to repeat it to us inexorably.
>
> When philosophers use a word—'knowledge', 'being', 'object', 'I', 'proposition', 'name'—and try to grasp the *essence* of the thing, one must always ask oneself: is the word ever actually used this way in the language-game which is its original home?—What *we* do is to bring words back from their metaphysical to their everyday use.
>
> [Emphases in original]

So: thinking that words such as 'simple' and 'composite' name attributes of 'objects' rather than being forms of understanding of the world; logically induced blindness to the multiplicity of words and their use; illusory attachment to an *a priori* order of 'super-concepts' which turn out (apparently) not be 'super' at all, but perfectly humble and ordinary; mistaking linguistic frames of reference for the nature of things; being captive to a picture repeated inexorably in language; and using words philosophically in (apparently) odd ways remote from their use in their 'home' language-games, then asking about the 'essences' which they name. At the very least this is no recommendation of the *Tractatus* philosophy!

Therefore, even if the AP is *not* simply a proxy for the philosophy of the *T*, for Wittgenstein there is clearly *some* connection between the two. For as he develops his critique of the AP he is happy to take 'side swipes' at the *T*, and clearly sees doing so as a legitimate *part* of his critique of the AP.

So what was this connection between the AP and the philosophy of the *T*? Typically, Wittgenstein never bothers to tell us, so we must speculate. But I think there is enough evidence in the *PI* to make such speculation at least informed speculation.

I think that, for the later Wittgenstein, the *T* is simply an *intellectualisation*—albeit a logically rigorous intellectualisation— of a set of underlying commonsense beliefs about language[3]— beliefs which he had simply taken as 'obvious truisms' or 'givens' when he wrote his early philosophy, and beliefs he thinks that the vast majority of human beings *still* treat as obvious, commonsense truisms. Moreover, it was because he thought that these underlying commonsense beliefs *were* so widespread and influential that, by the time he came to write his later philosophy, he was much more concerned to critique *them* than his intellectualisation of them.

And I think he was right about this in both senses: that is, he was right to believe that the assumptions critiqued in the *PI* are *very* widespread (they are found among many of the student theses analysed in this book, for example); and (therefore) he was also right to believe that critiquing them was a lot more important and significant than critiquing the *T per se*.

Prior to critiquing these assumptions, however, Wittgenstein attaches them (perhaps rather unfairly) to Augustine's name ('the Augustinian picture of language'). He does this for a typically perverse reason. Wittgenstein was a profound admirer of Augustine—he thought him a truly great thinker. Therefore if Augustine too shared what Wittgenstein had come to think were just 'prejudices' and 'superstitions' about language—if he too treated them as simply 'commonsense'—they must, Wittgenstein thought, be *profound* prejudices and superstitions, which are really hard—incredibly hard—to see through.

So what *are* these obvious 'truisms' now seen by Wittgenstein as dubious and obscuring 'superstitions'? Wittgenstein tells us some of them in the very first remarks in the *PI* reproduced above—the ones he makes immediately after the quotation from Augustine's *Confessions*.

(1) Every word has a meaning.
(2) This meaning is correlated with the word.

(3) The meaning of a word is the object for which it stands.

But as the *PI* unfolds at least two other AP truisms-superstitions—emerge.

(4) Every word has an *essential* or *primary* meaning from which all other meanings are derived, and which remains fixed throughout its uses.

(5) Meanings are attached to words by a mental act (precisely the act of 'meaning' them).

Belief (5) may seem to be in conflict with belief (3) but in fact it is not, because in the AP the primary way that we mean a word is to attach it to 'the object for which it stands' by a 'mental act' (the act of 'meaning' it) inside our heads.

By the end of the *PI*, however, Wittgenstein has shown—or thinks he has shown—that:

■ every word has not *one* meaning, but several or multiple meanings, depending on how it is used;

■ words *do* get meaning by standing for objects, but they also get meaning in many other ways that have nothing to do with standing for objects;

■ words *may* have essential or primary meanings but those meanings do *not* remain fixed throughout all their other uses; and

■ *sometimes* we mean words by mental acts, but such mental acts are not necessary for words to have meaning. Usually we mean words by *using* them in appropriate contexts, and we can do that without there being *any* mental act of 'meaning' them that accompanies or precedes such use.

Now it is undoubtedly the third of the *PI* theses above that most people find the most difficult to swallow. That is to say, most readers of the *PI* who have previously been 'in thrall' (as Wittgenstein puts it) to the AP, can be persuaded that there does not have to be one meaning for each word, that words get meanings in ways other than standing for objects, even that we can mean words without having to experience a mental act of 'meaning' every time. But by far the most common form of scepticism about the *PI* relates to Wittgenstein's claim to have shown that it is simply a 'prejudice' or 'superstition' to believe that there is an essential meaning of 'tree' (for example) which remains at play even in such 'extended' or 'projected' uses of the word as, say, 'family tree'.

Even the most open-minded and sympathetic readers of the *PI* have had difficulty dumping the AP belief that there *must* be something in common to all uses of the word 'tree' (or 'game', or 'table', or 'politics' or 'justice'). Because, or so they reason, if there was not this common link these things would not be called 'trees', 'tables', 'politics', etc., in *all* uses. And if that is so, then while it may be true that the word 'tree' can be *used* in all kinds of ways—ways which have nothing to do with botany, plants, bark or sap (for example, 'family tree', 'shoe tree')—those figurative or extended uses still depend, at bottom, on an essential or original meaning. Hence the meaning of words cannot, or at least cannot *always*, be identified with the uses of words.[4] 'At bottom' use depends on meaning, not the other way round.

Wittgenstein tried to deal with this objection through the idea of 'family resemblance'. Wittgenstein uses this idea (along with the analogy of 'strands of fibre in a rope') to suggest that, while there are indeed connections between, say, a botanical tree and a family tree, they work in such a way that the word 'tree' in 'family tree' has *no* direct connection to its original meaning.

Thus, botanical trees have trunks and branches. The ideas of a 'trunk' and 'branches' appear analogically in the concept of a family tree: the 'trunk' represents an original kinship or family 'stem' or 'line', which then 'branches' in dyadic ways. Moreover, as those branches divide and redivide through time, they can be physically drawn in such a way that the 'family tree' develops ever smaller branches ('twigs') and even 'leaves'. However if, when you have taken the connections this far, you then try to make a *direct* connection *back* to the original meaning (as in 'Can I carve my initials in the bark of the family tree?' or 'How long do its seeds take to germinate?', or 'Will you give me a cutting off the family tree so I can plant it out?') you will either be making a rather feeble joke or talking nonsense. According to Wittgenstein this shows that there is no original or essential meaning of the word 'tree' ('the object for which it stands') that remains fixed or constant throughout *all* its uses and is 'still there', as it were, in 'family tree'. In other words, family trees have 'trunks' and 'branches' and perhaps even 'leaves', but they don't grow in anything, they don't require watering, their seeds don't germinate, i.e., they are just not trees in the original sense.

Even so, doesn't the meaning of 'family tree' still depend, in some sense, on the original botanical meaning of the word 'tree'? Well yes, but the sense, or the way, in which it 'depends' on the original meaning is itself determined by how we use that original meaning as we extend or project the concept. In the case of 'family tree', for example, we keep the original elements of trunks and branches, but we dump or ignore sap, roots, photosynthesis, germination, fertilisation, shade, soil, and a host of other tree-related phenomena. And moreover, the trunk and branches we have kept are very peculiar arboreally speaking. The branches of a family tree do branch from a trunk, but they don't snap or bend, or blow in the wind or get nested in by birds.

In short, how the extended meaning 'depends' on the original meaning is itself determined by how we extend the concept, which means how we put it to new conceptual use. New meaning depends on new use, not on old meaning.

To use one of Wittgenstein's analogies, it is like the way fibres of hemp or nylon are spun together to make up a rope. In the act of spinning, the fibres are twisted together to make up the strands of the rope and one end of the rope *is*, as a result, connected to the other end (the new concept *is* connected to the original concept). But the connection is indirect, i.e. there is no *single* fibre (no single meaning) *which runs right though the rope* from one end to the other.[5]

But as the *PI* unfolds, it becomes clear that Wittgenstein thinks that our understanding of language can be profoundly distorted, not only by the conception of the meaning of words found in the AP, but also by too much concentration on the meaning of (single) words. (What does 'freedom' mean? What does 'democracy' mean? What does 'justice' mean?). For as Wittgenstein stresses, words are put to use ('employed' or 'deployed') in sentences, propositions and paragraphs, etc., and it is often far more clarifying to ask what a sentence or a paragraph means than what individual words in the sentence or paragraph mean. For sentences, propositions, etc., provide shifting contexts for words, contexts that in turn often affect the meaning of individual words both subtly and profoundly.

In fact, by the time the analysis in the *PI* is completed, Wittgenstein has undermined the entire AP of language. Words are now presented as an enormously varied range of 'tools' or 'instruments' to be put to use, rather than a uniform set of things called 'words', to be defined or determined. The meanings of words are seen as 'open' or 'shifting' rather than as 'fixed' or closed by solid, impenetrable boundaries (their definitions). Precision and exactitude in language is seen as dependent on the shifting and various purposes of its users (exact or precise 'in what sense?', 'to do what?') rather than on some characteristic or attribute of the words themselves (for example, their tight, formal definition). Hence, while it may often be appropriate to be exact or precise with language, the way we go about doing this is very different from the way a definition-obsessed thinker in thrall to the AP would suggest.

You, the reader, must make up your own mind as to whether you are persuaded by all this. Quite clearly I am. But that is not my most important reason for turning aside from the main line of argument in this book and laying out some of the more difficult technical issues and debates around Wittgenstein's *PI* argument in this addendum. Rather my reason is the following.

If Wittgenstein's argument in the *PI* is correct, and *if* belief in some version of the AP *is* as widespread and deep as he thought—*if*, in particular, it is as enormously widespread in academia as I am predisposed to think—then breaking with it is a quite revolutionary thing to do. In fact, it is a far more intellectually revolutionary thing to do than following Foucault or Deleuze or Derrida down the paths of deconstruction and social construction of reality. For all these supposedly 'radical' theorists are as deeply 'in thrall' to the AP of language as are the more 'conventional' or 'conservative' academic thinkers and theorists (such as positivists, empiricists or essentialists) that they lambast.[6] And as I hope readers have seen from other chapters in this book, this thraldom has had, and continues to have, deeply damaging implications (of a mainly deterministic sort) for their whole intellectual—and political—project.

8. The last and most tangled knot: The linguistic construction of subjectivity

Undoubtedly one of the main intellectual appeals of the whole tradition of theorising I have been reviewing in this book is its contention that one of the 'things'—perhaps the most important or significant 'thing'—that language constructs is human subjectivity itself. One of the appeals of this idea is precisely that it seems to undermine the commonsense conclusion reached during the last chapter. Namely that what matters in society—what may imprison, oppress, liberate or empower people—is not language itself, but the use of language by people. (That is, when the use of language is just a part of oppressive, liberating, empowering activities in which people engage.)

The theoretical objection to this, however, is that who and what these people are, and indeed what they do—the activities they engage in—can only be described in language, with the result that (so it is said) to 'posit' people, or to posit 'essential subjects' outside of language is theoretically naïve.

'The Critique of the Subject': Origins

Although, as we have seen, most of the student authors identify this anti-essentialism about subjects with Foucault above all, it is in fact of rather older provenance. In France at least it can be traced back to the late 1960s/early 1970s, and to the work of the father of so-called 'structural Marxism'—Louis Althusser—who was, among other things, the teacher of Foucault, Derrida, Deleuze and Guattari and a profound influence on the early work of Laclau and Mouffe.

This is not the place to introduce Althusser's ideas.[1] But it is important to understand that, while Foucault and the others eventually rejected their teacher's attempt to reconstruct Marxism as a form of structuralism (and in that sense they are poststructuralists), they never abandoned, indeed they whole-heartedly embraced and reiterated, his violent and thorough-going opposition to 'philosophical humanism' in general and to what he termed 'the problematic of the subject' in particular.

Since Althusser's reasons for rejecting all talk about 'essential subjects' are more or less identical to those of Foucault, Deleuze etc., they do not require separate intellectual treatment here and can be taken as encompassed in the critique that follows. Nonetheless I want to draw attention, briefly, to Althusser at the beginning of this chapter partly because he has been forgotten—he seems unknown to all but two of the student authors in my sample for example—and partly because, as I have said, it is he, *not* Foucault, who deserves 'credit' (if that be the word) for founding 'the critique of the subject' in French intellectual life. But I also draw attention to him to try to demonstrate that his work, and therefore that critique, emerged from a uniquely, almost farcically, low point in the history of high intellectual French Marxism, and that its profound weaknesses reflect that fact. I will outline very briefly here what I mean by this. (Those wishing more detail are directed to the readings on Althusser listed in the notes to this chapter.)

Althusser's original assault on 'the problematic of the subject' was just one aspect of his critique of the official Marxism of the 1960s French Communist Party. In constructing that critique, Althusser convicted both Marx himself and the French Communist Party of something he called economic 'reductionism'. He also convicted the early Marx (but not the later 'scientific' Marx) of 'naïve humanism' and the European communist movement in general of never having transcended that humanism. But since Althusser's account of the later Marx's economic reductionism was deeply philosophically confused,[2] and his account of the early Marx's humanism highly question-begging, they led him, in tandem, to adopt a kind of 'mirror-image' *linguistic* determinism (under the title 'structural Marxism'), as their combined antidote. That is, in 'structural Marxism' 'reductionism' was avoided by treating the economic realm, and the material realm in general, as linguistic constructs, and 'naive humanism' was avoided by treating human subjects as also entirely linguistically produced. Moreover, in developing his critique of Marx and offering his 'structuralist' alternative, Althusser not only proffered and popularised (through his students) a number of very debatable theses about Marx's own thought,[3] he also originated a uniquely ugly, syntactically tortured, 'theoretical' prose style which—also by being perpetuated in the writings of his students—has continued to exert enormous influence long after the texts in which it was first embodied have been forgotten.[4]

I want to emphasise then that the student authors whose work is surveyed in this book are the entirely unwitting inheritors of, perpetuators of, and indeed victims of, a radical linguistic or idealist determinism that first took wing in Paris about 40 years ago. They are therefore both the product and the victim of a highly dubious episode in French intellectual history, but an episode about which they are never taught (sometimes because their own teachers do not know it). Indeed they are, I believe, the victims of this history in good part *because* they are never taught it. They have, for example, no idea that their supposed poststructuralism, far from constituting a radical break with 'structuralist' Marxism, is, at least in its most radically idealist and determinist dimension, virtually a linear *continuation* of it.

'The Critique of the Subject' as a One-Sided Diet

In any event, whether found in Althusser, Foucault or Deleuze, it is quite clear what gives 'anti-essentialism' about subjects, and 'the critique of the subject' based upon it, some *a priori* plausibility. This is, that if we think of the single words and phrases we use to describe people—including ourselves—*man*, *woman*, *child*, *American*, *Russian*, *alien*, *asylum seeker*, *Asian*, *European*, *Moslem*, *terrorist*, then:

- they are clearly all 'words', so all part of 'language' and, more importantly
- such words often have social, political or ethical connotations (think of the phrase 'of Middle Eastern appearance', for example)—connotations that may be extremely influential in the way in which people think of themselves, or others think of and (thus) treat them. Moreover,
- when we describe human activities in such ways as (say) *typically female* or *manly* or *alien and unAustralian* or *typically Asian* we are not just describing these activities but 'stereotyping' them (and those who engage in or are affected by them) in ways which—again—can have important implications for the ways in which people are treated and indeed treat themselves.

I hope that now, and especially in the light of the Wittgensteinian ideas about language surveyed in the previous chapter, we can see that the notion that 'language constructs subjectivity' is not so much false (for all the observations above are, in a certain sense, true) as 'a partial truth' whose partiality derives from its 'one-sided diet of examples'.[5] And by this I mean both a one-sided diet of examples of language use and a one-sided diet of types of human activity surrounding that language use.

Thus I can say, 'I can't do that, it's unmanly', but I can also say, 'I don't care whether or not they think it's unmanly, it's the appropriate thing to do here.'

Thus I can say, 'Isn't it disgusting to see a man dressed like that, and behaving like a woman,' or I can say 'I wonder what its like to do that? Maybe I'll try, it might help.'

Thus I can say, 'He was of Middle Eastern appearance and clearly up to no good,' or I can say 'What the hell do you mean "of Middle Eastern appearance"? First, I'm not sure you'd know, and second I happen to know why he was there. He's a Brazilian friend of mine who was waiting for me to pick him up from the underground car park.'

Thus I can say, 'It was a typically Asian, sneaky way of going on,' or I can say 'I have no idea what "typically Asian" is supposed to mean. I know seven or eight people well, all of whom could be classified as Asian, but they are as individually different as any other group of eight people I know. Seems like an empty stereotype to me.'

In each of these cases what I say is no guide to what I *mean*, unless something more is known about how, why and when I say it. Thus, in the first set of alternatives I may be being homocentric, homophobic and racist, or I may be being ironic, and (say) endeavouring to uncover or lampoon the homocentricity, homo-phobia and racism of others. In the second set of alternatives, I may be engaged in a serious struggle against homophobia or racism, etc., but equally I may be being hypocritical, or manifesting 'cheap' virtue in the safe confines of a university classroom, or just making a philosophical argument. It all depends on what else I am doing while/when (or before, or after) I am saying it.

However that may be, it is clear that when we move away from a focus on 'identity-defining'—or supposedly identity-defining— words and phrases, and focus instead on the use of those words and phrases in what philosophers call 'speech acts'[6] then we see what is obvious—the same words and phrases can be used in ways that are identity-defining, identity-challenging, identity-melding or identity-questioning. In other words, and contrary to very commonly encountered assertions, *alien*, *asylum seeker*, *of Middle Eastern appearance, a typical man, a very untypical woman, a totally camp queer darling* are not—they *are* not—stereotypes, although they may be used as such. Equally they are not—they *are* not—*not* stereotypes, although they may be used to challenge and subvert stereotypes (and create new ones, and subvert them, then create more, and, and, and . . .).

However, one way to deny what is said above is by questioning all the 'I can say's' above. What, precisely, I might ask, does 'can' mean in such assertions? What if, for example, even saying 'maybe I'll try [cross-dressing]' means I am socially ostracised or even violently assaulted? What if even thinking such things produces violent feelings of guilt or self-revulsion in me? In such cases 'can' I really say or think such things, even if, formally, my language allows me to say or think them?

A good and important question, but surely the very way the question is posed suggests its answer—that other people may use their power over me to prevent me speaking or, even worse, I may—through fear, or cowardice, or emotional or ethical confusion—censor or suppress my own words, thoughts and desires. But in either case it is not language or discourse that is exerting the power, or producing the self-censorship or suppression. It is the actions of people—either of other people, or of 'me myself'. The solution to such forms of oppression and suppression is not, therefore, any change of language (or certainly not 'in and of itself') but, in the first case active resistance to the power of others and, in the second, finding the strength to overcome or resolve my fears and confusions.

Now, changing some form or bits of language could play a role in both types of struggle, and we know from the history of virtually every radical political movement that it often does. Again, however, the important point is this: if people need to change any form or piece of language for any purpose then it can be changed—it offers no resistance whatsoever to such change, no matter how radical the change might be. It is other users of language—other people—who may, and often do, offer such resistance. And then the struggle is on.

In short, it makes about as much sense to say that 'language constructs identity' (or 'subjectivity') as it makes to say that 'tools construct kitchen cabinets'—that is, it makes some sense, but not much. Yes, sometimes, some tools are used to construct kitchen cabinets. But the same tools can be used to smash up kitchen cabinets, turn kitchen cabinets into toys, or move a kitchen cabinet into the garden and use it as a dog kennel. Similarly, words and phrases can be used to stereotype people. They can even be used by people to stereotype themselves. But they can also be used to resist and subvert stereotypes, reinforce or explore a new sense of self or identity, and to accompany a total nervous breakdown in which all sense of self is lost.

Addendum
Wittgenstein's conception of language as a city, or theory as intellectual laziness

As I said in Chapter 6, Wittgenstein himself was rather leery of characterising 'language as a whole'. And the reason for this is that he thought any attempt to say what language 'was' (as an entity) obscured what we most needed to understand about it—namely that it isn't any kind of entity! But of course that proposition itself is, or certainly seems, self-contradictory. For if I say that 'language' or 'it' isn't 'any kind of entity', then I can properly be asked what, if this is true, the words 'language' and 'it' mean in the sentence above.

Therefore Wittgenstein's most common brief answer to the question of what language 'is' is 'a collection'—i.e., a large bunch of words that can be used in the enormously varied contexts of human life in almost any way we want—just as the tools in a tool shed are a large and various collection of things that are both intended for and can be put to very various uses, some/many of them beyond those intended.

Interestingly, on the rare occasions when he did present a more developed analogy for language, Wittgenstein favoured that of an unplanned old town or city, which has grown in an *ad hoc* or 'organic' way. In this city, different 'parts' or 'suburbs' or 'regions' are of very different ages and structures, differences that often reflect the various activities that go on in them (religion, poetry, law, natural science, mathematics, engineering, sport, etc.).[7]

I think it is fairly clear that this analogy seeks to invoke language as a 'home', as 'our' (in the most universal sense of 'our') home.

There could hardly be a more distant image, both intellectually and emotively, from the Foucauldian notion of language as a kind of inhuman power machine or industrial scape, in which both 'oppressor' and 'oppressed' are robotically dynamised by a set of 'power relations' that somehow they all 'share'. Language for Foucault may or may not be a prison (as some have claimed or complained), but it is most certainly not a home, not only in the sense that he presents it as very uncomfortable and incommodious, but in the more profound sense that there seems to be nobody living there (although there are 'bodies' moving about).

Analogies are analogies. They all more or less illuminate different aspects of reality—none are 'right' or 'wrong', 'correct' or 'incorrect'. But I certainly think Wittgenstein's analogy of language to a city reminds us of many important things about the human condition.

- For good or ill we are all stuck together in our city— we've got nowhere else to go.
- Sometimes, some of us get on well there, but
- there are also frequent quarrels and disagreements— at worst some of them are violent.
- The population of the city is not a population of equals—profound and deep inequalities, and the use and abuse of power deriving from those inequalities, are pervasive. Nonetheless,
- sometimes things get worked out and improved. But, in any event,
- things go on—the city does not care. Although,
- depending on what does go on, it may get wholly or partially burned down, restructured, rebuilt and added to. And one thing is for certain,
- the city does not, in itself, 'determine' anything that goes on there, although it may sometimes 'shape' or 'influence' it (if we let it!).

The most important point about Wittgenstein's analogy of language with an 'organically' grown town or city is that the analogy is always presented from a perspective from the streets of the city.

> Our language can be seen as an ancient city: a maze of little streets and squares, of old and new houses, and of houses with additions from various periods, and this surrounded by a multitude of new boroughs with straight regular streets and uniform houses. *PI,* 18

And, much more explicitly:

> In teaching you philosophy I'm like a guide showing you how to find your way around London. I have to take you through the city from north to south, from east to west, from Euston to the Embankment and from Piccadilly to Marble Arch. After I have taken you on many journeys through the city, in all sorts of directions, we shall have passed through a given street a number of times—each time traversing the street as part of a different journey. At the end of this you will know London: you will be able to find your way about like a born Londoner.[8]

In another book I noted the close similarity between what Wittgenstein says in the second quotation above and the way that London taxi drivers acquire what they refer to as 'The Knowledge'—their memorised command of a vast range of travel routes around London.[9] Traditionally, apprentice cabbies learned these routes by riding them on a bicycle, memorised them and then took an oral exam conducted by a qualified cabbie who could ask them about any route—e.g., 'What's the fastest likely route from Holborn Tube to Heathrow airport at the peak period?'

The point about this kind of knowledge of routes (and of different parts of London) is that it is not acquired from a map or street atlas, and still less from Google Earth, or some other kind of aerial survey. Rather it is acquired entirely 'at ground level' as it were.

Analogously, and to return to the first quotation for a moment, Wittgenstein learns, and wanted his students to learn, about the 'maze of little streets and squares' by visiting each and every one of them, and to learn about the 'new boroughs with straight regular streets and uniform houses' (the specialist languages of mathematics and natural science for example) by making regular visits there. Or rather, and to abandon the analogy for a moment, Wittgenstein wanted his students to join him in an exhaustive examination of detailed examples of language use. And—back to the analogy—exploring these examples can be compared, not just to a visit to the 'maze of little streets', but to a particular corner of a particular street, to a particular side alley not even seen on a previous visit, or to a beautiful little Georgian square almost hidden behind some huge modern tower block.

The point of this is that:

■ there is no way of knowing, *a priori* as it were, what you will find on any given visit (or certainly not in detail); and

■ 'ground level' visits often reveal what no map or aerial survey will show so well or clearly, or in such detail.

That is the thrust of such remarks as:

> We do not command a clear view of our use of language. Our grammar is lacking in that kind of perspicuity.
> *PI*, 122

Or, in more detail:

> The criteria which we accept for 'fitting', 'being able to', 'understanding' are much more complicated than might appear at first sight. That is, the game with these words, their employment in the linguistic intercourse that is carried on by their means, is more involved—the role of these words in our language is other—than we are tempted to think.
>
> (The role is what we need to understand in order to resolve philosophical paradoxes. And hence definitions usually fail to resolve them; and so, *a fortiori*, does the assertion that they are 'indefinable'.) *PI*, 182

And as I hope is by now clear, Wittgenstein thinks that we will never get a 'clear view' of 'our use of language' from some vast aerial survey (from the vacuous abstract assertion, for example, that 'all words signify something'). In other words, the reason we are 'tempted', 'at first sight' to think things about 'the role of . . . words in our language'—things which turn out to be over-simplified or just plain wrong—is that we just haven't made the visits, or enough visits, to different parts of the city. We haven't done the hard yards—worked the examples of language use, or enough examples in enough detail. Instead we have opted for the passingly plausible, but in fact just lazy, generalisation, which puffs itself up as a great 'theoretical' insight. Such generalisations might include, 'In the end, language gets its meaning from picturing the world' or 'There *has* to be something to which every word corresponds or no word would have a meaning'. (Oh yes? So what do 'Help!' or 'You don't say?' correspond to?)

And the reason that we must avoid this kind of 'abstractive' theoretical laziness is that 'in the end' the analogy between language and a city breaks down in a crucial way. (This in itself is not a problem. All analogies break down, if they didn't they wouldn't be analogies.)

Wittgenstein's analogy breaks down because one cannot make an aerial survey or a detailed street map of language 'from outside' or 'from above' in the way that one can of even the largest, most sprawling, city, because language is more like the universe. We human beings simply cannot get 'outside' it or 'above' it. Therefore we have to learn about language purely 'from street level', as it were, by exploring it, inch by inch, on foot or on a bicycle, by making endless visits and revisits, and by taking copious notes. And, needless to say, this task can never be completed because language, like the city, is growing and changing all the time—new suburbs are added, old ones demolished or refashioned, streets are widened or rerouted. And given all this, I find nothing more extraordinary in all the student theses with which I am concerned in this book than their easy and confident assertions that something called *language* (often with a capital 'L') *has enormous power* or *is* this or that, or *does* this or that, or *constructs* or *determines* this or that. In every case, I want to ask, 'How on earth do you know?!'

But does the fact that we cannot 'escape' language, any more than we can 'escape' the universe—that we must always 'map' or 'explore' it from 'inside'—make language a prison, or give it the 'power' to 'determine' anything of any importance to human beings? Well perhaps this final analogy provides the answer. We cannot escape the universe either, but, at least to date, this has never stopped human beings doing anything that they want to do! The universe is huge and (apparently) growing all the time and it has many dangerous places and forces. But it is our home and, if nothing else, it has space enough and resources enough for us to do almost anything in it—as long, of course, as we learn how to use, and not abuse, those resources.

PART III

good causes and bad philosophy

9. Confusion and virtue

In this book's Introduction, I said:

> The real damage done by the kind of ideas I survey in this book is not felt on those rarefied academic heights where luminaries of the *grandes écoles* joust with each other or their supporters and adversaries from Oxford, Harvard or Yale . . . The real damage occurs as a result of the 'trickle-down' of such ideas to lower levels of academe, where they gain students' allegiance more through considerations of status, fashion, political or ethical commitment to some notion or other of 'the good', and sheer undiluted confusion, than anything that can be remotely called rational argument.

I hope that the previous chapters have said enough about the 'sheer undiluted confusion'. It is not my intention in this book to give much attention to the 'considerations of status or fashion' beyond remarking, I suppose, that young people in particular are (and always have been) very vulnerable to the latter. As for status, well the status—or supposed status—of these ideas, especially for more able students, derives from their perceived difficulty and profundity. But the reputation of poststructuralist and postmodern theory for being difficult rests almost entirely on its arcane expression rather than on any genuine intellectual difficulty. I hope I have succeeded in showing that such theory is not at all profound. On the contrary, many of the most hallowed and oft-repeated poststructuralist maxims rest on the most shallow understanding of how human language works, a shallowness disguised only by opaque, jargon-istic expression.

So that leaves 'political or ethical commitment to some notion or other of the good', which is most certainly at play in all of the theses analysed in this book, as will be apparent to anyone who has read the quotations. The following is a more or less comprehensive list of the main political goals or objectives explicitly advanced in the theses.

1. Opposition to various expressions of western cultural imperialism: 'Orientalism'; the construction of Africa as 'the Dark Continent'; and the requirement, especially in 'realist' international relations writings, that all states function in an identical manner. (POLS/IR 4 and 5, POLS/IR 9 to 12)

2. Defence of the Acehnese people's independence struggle in Indonesia. (POLS/IR 3)

3. Defence of anarchist conceptions of the State (as an always oppressive political and ideological force), against 'realist' forms of international relations discourse that assert, or just assume, its 'naturalness' or normalcy. (POLS/IR 10)

4. Opposition to oppressive and racist treatment of refugees and asylum seekers, both by the Australian state and other states. (POLS/IR 14 to 18)

5. Opposition to construction of sex, gender and (thus) of female and male identity in standard or dominant (i.e. sexist) discourse. (POLS/Fem 1 to 4)

6. Opposition to discourses of 'essential' ethnic or cultural difference, discourses which deny the possibility of individuals having and negotiating 'hybrid' identities. (POLS/IR 13)

7. Opposition to the illiberal effects of the deployment of Cold War rhetoric, especially in the context of the Vietnam War. (POLS/Misc 3)

8. Opposition to the ridiculing of 'the artist, the conservationist and the intellectual' in 'mechanisms of mass communication'. (POLS/Misc 5, p. 19)

Now I am very sympathetic to some of these political objectives (notably 4, 7 and 8), sympathetic with qualifications to most of the others (1, 2, 5 and 6) and entirely unsympathetic to one (3), but neither my sympathy nor my hostility plays any role in what I want to say in the rest of this chapter. For what I want to say is simply that the construction of strong and persuasive arguments in favour of any or all of these positions or objectives does not require the use of the 'theoretical' apparatus and arguments found in all these theses. Indeed, in many cases and respects, the political force of students' arguments are severely weakened or compromised by the use of this theory.

There are many reasons for this, but the most important is also the most obvious.

It is quite possible, and often relatively easy, to show that a human being A, or a group of human beings B (including a state or states), is using some bit, or form, or aspect of language in a way or manner that is contemptuous of, or vilifies, or stereotypes, another human being C, or group of human beings D (including a state or states). But showing this empirically to be the case does not require onc to assert that an entity called 'language' or 'discourse' is in and of itself—in its essence as it were—contemptuous, or vilifying, or stereotyping.

Similarly, it is quite possible, and often relatively easy, to show that a human being A, or a group of human beings B, are using some bit, or form, or aspect of language to describe and understand themselves in ways that are—arguably—damaging to them. But showing this empirically to be the case does not require one to assert that an entity called 'language' or 'discourse' is in and of itself—in its essence as it were—damaging or destroying identity or subjectivity.

In short then, all the student authors reviewed in this book could have made their political arguments perfectly satisfactorily in a much less generalised and more empirically focused manner, without the 'theory' of which they are so enamoured. Further, in so far as they either make untrue theoretical or philosophical claims prior to their empirical analysis and then claim that the latter is based on them, or (worse) argue that their empirical analysis validates the spurious 'theoretical' claims (when it clearly does not and could not), they weaken the political force of their argument. In short, then, the theory deployed in all these theses is both redundant to their political claims and (at least tangentially) damaging to them.

This of course assumes that all the student authors are serious when they make their more dramatic, or even melodramatic, theoretical claims—that they are being intellectually serious when they say, for example, 'identity is produced through variable forces and discursive fields', or 'in effect, discourse produces the world' or 'the "real world" is created by language', or 'all institutional arrangements . . . are discursively constructed' or 'language has incredible power to influence how issues are represented in the public arena' or 'there is no pre-discursive gender or sex' or 'prior to the call, there is no social subject'.

We could assume otherwise. We might adopt a principle of 'interpretive generosity', which treats such assertions as carelessly overblown prolegomena to empirical studies, or sees them as being justified (in the students' eyes) solely by the particular empirical case with which they are concerned. In short, we could assume that the student authors either have not given serious thought to the question of what is required for such assertions to be genuinely universally true, or even that they do not really intend them to be taken as universally true.[1] And if that were the case, then in this book I would be taking a massive philosophical hammer to smash what is, in reality, the softest of non-philosophical nuts.

The problem with such interpretive generosity in this case is that it carries an equal and opposite danger—that of being deeply patronising, of failing to take the students' own aspirations seriously. As I noted at the beginning of this book, the students who write the kind of theses reviewed in it typically take theory very seriously, are usually proud of the strong and developed theoretical dimension of their theses and certainly do not present theory as just a portentous generalisation of a specific political truth shown, or supposedly shown, by their empirical case study. They present theory as something more, and more important, than this. Most frequently in fact, they present their empirical case study or studies, as 'confirmation' of broader theoretical truths already known or established.

I therefore think that, on balance, one must avoid being patronising, and treat theory with the intellectual seriousness with which the students treat it—which means not treating it as mere overblown introductory rhetoric, or facile over-generalisation of a specific case or cases.

But if one treats theory as seriously as the students do, this leads one ultimately to an overwhelming question, hanging in the air throughout this book, but so far unanswered. 'What then is this sort of "theory"?' If, as I have argued above, it is not, on the one hand, any kind of aid to, or necessary prelude to, or requirement of, empirical analysis and, on the other, it is radically inadequate and untrue as philosophy of language, then what is it?

Well the answer, banal as it may seem, is that it is 'theory', and that this kind of theory is a sort of abortive semi-philosophy. Such theory rests on the (usually unstated) premise that before one can make particular empirical claims or findings one must first make universalist theoretical assertions (often called a 'theoretical context') 'within which', as it is usually put, the empirical analysis can be located. Thus one cannot, in this case, look at the actual use of language by specific people A in specific historical or geographical context B, until one has a 'general concept of language' or a 'general concept of discourse' to provide a theoretical context for the empirical discussion. But as I hope we have now seen, this is nothing more than a superstition dressed up as a methodological principle. Because

- the idea of a 'general concept of language or discourse' is itself just a confusion; and anyway
- language gets its meaning from its use (ditto 'discourse') not from its 'structure' (or some such); and therefore
- nothing you say about it (because it isn't an 'it') is going to tell you anything about how people use it.

Therefore, and fairly obviously, one can proceed directly to an empirical example, or examples, of language use, without any need for any 'theoretical' discussion about what language 'is', etc.

Actually, I think that what is true of language is true of virtually everything of importance that political scientists or social scientists wish to discuss. It is equally true, for example, of power, government, justice, rights, equality and inequality, states, culture, status, gender and class.

To demonstrate that the above assertions are true would take me well outside the scope of this book. (Although I hope what I have said in these chapters has given at least attentive readers an idea of the logic of the argument in all these cases.) But while I am dealing in unsubstantiated assertions I also want to say that, whether they know it or not, social scientists—even radical, unorthodox ones—labour under the superstition that theory must always precede, and provide the setting for, empirical analysis, from a spurious analogy of their own activity to some forms of natural science. That is, statements such as 'You can't know what an oak tree is until you know what a tree is' or 'You can't understand what a carbon atom is until you know what atoms are' may work in natural science—where we are indeed dealing with human understandings of a world of things. But they don't work in social science, simply because we are dealing with human understandings of others' purposive activities, and that makes a world of difference.

It makes a world of difference because it means that, being precisely purposive, the 'things' that social scientists study (human activities) are never exactly repeated. And because they are never exactly repeated, universalist assertions about them can never work. The most that social scientists can manage is broad-scale empirical generalisations about human activity, generalisations that are, indeed, often 'generally' true (i.e., true in a majority, even a large majority, of cases for some slice or other of human history). But empirical generalisations are just that—empirical generalisations. They do not require any body of 'theory' either to offer or validate them. They just need a good, sound empirical and historical knowledge of what people do.[2]

But still, why do I call theory 'abortive semi-philosophy'? I call it that because philosophy is itself an empirical generalisation about what people do—in this particular case about how they think and act with language. But the 'theory' presented in these theses presents itself as something more than that—it presents itself as an account of how people 'must' 'always' think and act with language (i.e., at all times and places). But there can be no such account, so of course 'theory' does not provide it. Rather, it simply presents a quick, crude set of *a priori* universalist assertions about 'language', but stops short of providing any worthwhile empirical generalisations about language use. (That is, such generalisations appear, if they appear at all, entirely in the theses' non-theoretical chapters.) So I think my characterisation of theory, or at least of the theory found in these theses, is both precise and accurate. It *is* abortive, and it *is* semi- (i.e., half-done) philosophy.

But whether this broader argument of mine is right or not, one thing is certain. Nobody needs theory to provide good arguments (or, for that matter, bad arguments) for good causes. As noted above, on the whole I approve of the causes for which many of the best students whom I teach want to argue. I believe, to use the conventional phrase, that those students have their hearts in the right place. And that is just the point I want to make. All they really need to make such arguments is a good heart, a good head and the willingness and ability to do hard empirical work. They don't need theory!

10. 'The Enlightenment project'

In the thesis POLS/IR 10 we find the following passages:

> George and Campbell have summarised some of the theoretical manifestations of this 'enlightenment project' as follows:

> 'its universalistic presuppositions about modern rational man, its metatheoretical commitment to dualised categories of meaning and understanding, its logocentric strategies of identity and hierarchy, its theorised propositions about human nature, its dogmatic faith in method, its philosophies of intention and consciousness and its tendency toward grand theory.' [Reference to J. George and D. Campbell, 'Patterns of dissent and the celebration of difference: Critical social theory and international relations', *International Studies Quarterly*, vol. 34, no. 3, 1990, p. 286]

The author of POLS/IR 10 then glosses this extract with a quote from Bernstein's *Beyond Objectivism and Relativism* thus:

> This metaphysic centres on 'the basic conviction that there must be some permanent, ahistorical matrix or

framework to which we can ultimately appeal in determining the nature of rationality, truth, reality, goodness
or rightness.' This framework presumes that explanations
will be true to the extent that they accurately reflect
empirical reality, to the extent that they correspond to the
facts. (1.4)

S/he then adds in his/her own words:

Considering the global dominance of western societies
culturally and politically over the recent past and present,
these values become instruments of dominating other
peoples, cultures and the natural world. Traditions
of liberalism and Marxism alike are rooted in the
'enlightenment project' of social, cultural and political
rationality . . . Western enlightenment philosophy thereby
creates a world of universals in order to imagine itself as
universal for the rest of the world.

And in the thesis POLS/Fem 2 we find the following extract:

Foucault's argument concerning the 'truth' or validity of
knowledge-claims is seen as quite disturbing by many
feminists. Firstly, it seems to imply relativism, which can
only serve to legitimate the status quo. A relativist stance
'accepts the dominant group's insistence that their right to
hold distorted views (and of course a policy for all of us on
the basis of those views) is intellectually legitimate' [quote
from K. Nash, 'The Feminist Production of Knowledge: Is
deconstruction a practice for Women?' *Feminist Review*,
no. 47, 1994, p. 70]. Secondly, Foucault's postmodern
deconstruction seems to lead to a denial of the relevance
of women's experience which has been the reference point
for the generation of feminist theorising and activism. If,
as Foucault argues, knowledge is always produced and

understood through power relations, and every account of the 'truth' is equal in its legitimacy, it seems impossible for there to exist a collective authentic or coherent voice of 'woman' based in any group of women's experiences of the world. Not only does Foucault's view of everything as discursively constructed imply that, for example, one gender is very much like another, that they're all equally constructed; but his argument that all human interests are also formed discursively, makes the claim that women are oppressed impossible. After all, what is to be liberated if all identities are discursively constructed? Furthermore, without the claim that women are oppressed, what would be the point, let alone impetus, of feminism?

The quotations from POLS/IR 10 are typical examples of a conception of the eighteenth-century European Enlightenment common not only in the student theses reviewed in this book, but among many scholars sympathetic to postmodernism. This is that the Enlightenment represents the beginning of a quintessentially 'western' worldview that has had generally damaging consequences for the world. That is to say, it has provided intellectual rationalisations for a variety of noxious deeds and developments—the European conquest and colonial exploitation of the non-European world, the technologically driven abuse of the world's environment and ecosystems, and a variety of oppressive regimes of 'discipline' and 'punishment' (be they penal, psychiatric or social)—both in the West itself and elsewhere.[1]

My aim in this brief chapter is not to consider in any systematic way the merits of this view (although I will say here that I consider it to be, at best, a half-truth—a half-truth broadly comparable to blaming Christ for the iniquities committed by Christians or Marx for all the horrors committed in the name of Marxism).

Rather, my aim is to consider the Enlightenment, not as

a historical phenomenon with historical (or alleged historical) consequences, but as an important philosophical movement and moment in history. I will suggest that the moment was distinguished both by great intellectual heroism and by very great danger, and that fashionable postmodernist strictures on 'the Enlightenment project' seriously underestimate both the heroism and the danger. I also hope to show that the current standard hostility to 'the Enlightenment project' often leads to a postmodernist 'politics of truth' (a politics perfectly represented by the quotation from POLS/Fem 2 above), which, in contrast with the Enlightenment itself, is not at all intellectually heroic. More importantly, it is also not remotely adequate to meeting the dangers posed by Enlightenment philosophy.

To put it simply, this danger arises from Enlightenment thinkers' insistence that truth and the consequences of truth should be kept absolutely distinct—both conceptually and emotionally. They should be kept so distinct because, logically, no assertion about the consequences (positive or negative) of a truth claim can have any implications for the truth value of that claim. The following four examples will bring this out clearly. In each of them the first assertions are standard postmodernist critiques of the 'Enlightenment project' and the 'Responses' (which are logically and semantically identical) are the classical Enlightenment repostes to such critiques.

1. 'The enlightenment doctrine that beliefs based on "reason" and "science" are superior to beliefs based on "religion" and "superstition" has been used to justify cultural contempt of non-western societies, and processes of imperialist conquest and cultural domination.'

Response:
'Yes, but is that doctrine true?'

2. 'The enlightenment belief that reason, and the science based on it, can be used to understand and control nature and natural forces has led to destructive abuse of the world's ecosystems and the current environmental crisis.'

Response:
'Yes, but is such a belief true?'

3. 'The belief that there are "natural", biological and evolutionary differences between the sexes has been used to justify a wide range of gender inequalities and oppressions.'

Response:
'Yes, but is such a belief true?'

4. 'The belief that there are "natural", biological and evolutionary differences among different human "races" has been used to justify various forms of racial discrimination, oppression and even genocide.'

Response:
'Yes, but is such a belief true?'

So we see that it is always possible to ask, in response to any proposition stating that a belief has had X or Y, social, political, cultural or environmental consequences, whether, nonetheless, the belief itself is true. That is, to say that beliefs A, B or C may have had pernicious consequences X, Y or Z, tells us nothing, in and of itself, about whether beliefs A, B and C are true. Indeed, the fact that beliefs A, B or C may have had desirable consequences X, Y or Z also tells us nothing, in and of itself, about whether beliefs A, B and C are true.

The social (or political or environmental) 'consequences'

of a belief tell us nothing, in and of themselves, about its truth because:

- a belief may be true, but its truth may have been 'misunderstood' or 'misconstrued' by those who have acted upon it (and have thus produced the consequences), *or*
- the alleged consequences may not be consequences of the belief at all, but developments or outcomes produced by some other factor or factors entirely, *or*
- the belief may be false, but acting upon it may have 'accidentally', or by good fortune, produced some desirable consequences.[2]

Obviously, to make a distinction between the truth of a proposition and its consequences immediately raises the issue of how, if not by its consequences, we may discover whether it is true, and here I would be absolutely philosophically orthodox. One discovers whether any proposition is true by examining the empirical evidence for and against it. That is, propositions are true if there is evidence to support them and/or no evidence to refute them, and they are false if there is no evidence to support them and/or there is evidence to refute them.

In fact of the four propositions considered above only two— the first two—derive specifically from the eighteenth-century European enlightenment. The first of these mainly functioned as a critique of Christian theology—which the Enlightenment thinkers believed to have no evidence to support it other than biblical authority, and which they thought should be replaced in human efforts to understand the natural and social worlds by the untrammelled use of human reason. Most of the Enlightenment thinkers also probably endorsed the second belief, which they took to mean that human beings could obtain a better control over (or at least mitigate the more disastrous effects of) those natural forces that afflicted them (for example, weather, pests and disease), by the use of reason rather than prayer or magical practices (the predominant approaches in Europe to such matters from time immemorial).[3]

Now, personally, I believe both these beliefs to be true—which is to say, I believe they both have considerable empirical evidence to support them. I believe that human beings do have a better understanding of both the natural and social world now, as a result of the application of science and reason, than they did when they allowed certain sacred texts to constrain that understanding. I also believe that, as a result of this improved understanding, human beings have gained better control over a range of human, animal and plant pests and diseases (though not over the weather) than they had before such serious attempts at understanding were made.[4]

But of course both these 'Enlightenment' propositions being true is perfectly compatible with their truth being used (wrongly) to justify the moral or cultural 'superiority' of western culture to other cultures, or to justify other forms of intervention in the natural environment that have had very damaging consequences.

But what this shows us—and this is very important—is that true propositions, at least in part because of their truth, can make very powerful raw material for political ideologies. They do so just because it is easier to make persuasive extrapolations from truths to various forms of half-truth or untruth. For example, from the (true) proposition that reason and science were celebrated by a certain group of intellectuals in Europe at one moment in history you can extrapolate the proposition that reason and science are therefore some kind of European invention or monopoly, which is untrue, both historically and culturally.[5] Or from the (true) proposition that certain specific applications of natural science have been of great benefit to humanity and to the natural environment you can extrapolate the (manifestly false) proposition that therefore any and all applications of natural science must be beneficial to both.

And this is why I added the 'non-Enlightenment' propositions about gender and race to the list above. For although such propositions have been widely believed in the West, the fourth is false (there are *no* biologically based human 'races' and, therefore, no hierarchy of races), and the third, though not specifically an Enlightenment proposition, is true (there is a biological basis to human sexual difference) but this truth does not justify the forms of gender inequality and oppression it has been used to justify. (And indeed quite different kinds of beliefs—notably religious beliefs about God's will—have been used to justify the same or similar forms of gender inequality and oppression). For this reason, the third belief, in part because it has been proven false, does not these days provide the powerful raw material for racist ideology it once did. And the fourth proposition, while true, is 'restrictedly' true and does not, if properly understood, provide much support for forms of gender inequality—a point that has been clearly grasped and politically used (by feminists and their supporters) in at least some of the world's societies.

So, true beliefs can be politically used and abused, false beliefs can be politically used and abused, and in both cases the use (if not the abuse—which usually derives from over-generalisation of some specific proposition) can have consequences we may regard as politically and/or ethically positive or negative.

But all this only confirms that the truth or falsity of propositions is one issue and the political use and abuse of them quite another, and the most courageous and dangerous philosophical aspect of the Enlightenment was just its rigid insistence on this point. Bacon (rather earlier), and in the eighteenth century Voltaire, Hume, Kant and Rousseau, all insisted that the investigation of a proposition's truth should be kept completely and absolutely distinct from any consideration of what the political, social, even personal, implications of its being true (or false) might be. And, moreover, the more contentious or explosive those implications, the more important they believed it to be to maintain this distinction.

Thus: either God exists, or he does not exist. This is a matter of fact to be established. To consider what would follow (in any realm of human life) if he does not exist (or if he does) is a separate question.

Thus: the earth was either created 10,000 years ago or it was not. This is a matter of fact to be established. To consider what might follow for the belief system of certain Christian fundamentalists if it is false (or true) is a separate question.

Thus: *homo sapiens* and certain great apes either share a common evolutionary ancestor or they do not. This is a matter of fact to be established. To consider what might follow for the belief system of all those who believe the human life form to be *sui generis* if it is true (or false) is an entirely separate question.

Thus: the brains of human females are either identical to the brains of human males or they are not. This is a matter of fact to be established. To consider what might be the implications for gender relations, or feminist politics, or anything else if it is false (or true) is an entirely separate question.

Thus: Jews and Australian Aboriginals are either lower races in some evolutionary hierarchy of human races or they are not. This is a matter of fact to be established. To consider what might follow for the welfare of either of these groups of human beings if it is true (or false) is an entirely separate question.

I have deliberately chosen the contentious or momentous examples above—examples whose truth or falsity has been of enormous social, political, even emotional, significance for many people—precisely because it is in such cases that maintaining the complete separation postulated above is so difficult. Nobody has any difficulty maintaining the separation in the case of 'the boiling point of water is either 100 degrees Celsius or it is not' or 'sodium is either dissoluble in hydrochloric acid or it is not', and very few people will have any difficulty with 'Pluto is either a planet in the solar system or it is not.' Moreover, even in the contentious/momentous examples above, some will be contentious/momentous to some people, and others will be contentious/momentous to others. But this is just the point. The central Enlightenment prescription is— and to repeat—'the more contentious/momentous it is *to you*, the more *you* should endeavour to maintain the absolute distinction'.

It is precisely this Enlightenment prescription that the vast majority of human beings find so hard to accept or, even if they accept it 'in principle', so very hard to act upon consistently. Indeed, I think it is debatable whether human beings should consistently act upon it, or at least in every case.

To see why, let us imagine some horrible absurdities, just because they are both horrible and absurd.

Ten thousand fierce believers in Enlightenment values are waiting outside the gas chambers. They are waiting just to get the results of the final conclusive tests in racial biology being conducted by Herr Himmler's scientists. The results come through and they are definitive. Jews are scientifically proven to be *untermenschen*. Ten thousand people sigh, shrug their shoulders and march obediently to their deaths.

Or, a breeding programme to eliminate Aboriginals genetically is being planned by the colonial government of New South Wales. All the Aboriginal people involved have agreed to take part in the programme if scientific testing currently being commissioned by the Colonial Office in London, and being carried out at the University of Edinburgh, proves that they are indeed on the lowest rung of the evolutionary hierarchy. The telegram comes though from London. The news is definitive . . . the programme begins, etc.

Surely when one considers examples such as this (chosen because they are uncomfortably close to historical truth) one *wants* to say 'Never mind whether this horrible proposition is true or not' or (better still), 'Fuck this proposition. It is so horrible and utterly unacceptable in its implications that even the attempt to find out if it is true or not should be violently resisted.'

Fortunately there is historical evidence that, put in this kind of situation, the vast majority of people do think and feel this way. But we should note that what they are saying is that they don't care whether these propositions are true or not because they are so ethically/humanly horrible. And they might also say that the very attempt to discover whether such propositions are true or false is itself so horrible that it should not be engaged in. What they are not saying (actually) is that *because* these propositions are ethically/humanly horrible they aren't true. And it is a very good thing that they are not saying this because if they were they would (for what little it would matter to them) be making a serious philosophical mistake.[6]

This mistake consists in equating what is true with what is convenient to some ethical, political, or religious worldview, or with what is in the interests of some group of human beings (including their 'interest' in staying alive!). And this equation is such a grave philosophical mistake to make (for those of us who are not facing extermination or genocide, and therefore have the luxury of thinking calmly and unhurriedly about these things) because it involves nothing less than a total evisceration of the concept of truth itself. For simply to be meaningful, this concept requires a complete, 'in principle' distinction between truth and preference. As we quite rightly say, 'If it is true it is true, whether I like it or not, or whether you like it or not—and whatever its consequences may be.' And we also say, equally rightly, 'If it is true it is true, whether anybody likes it or not.' This means, also, that 'If it is true, it is true for everybody' and 'If it is false, it is false for everybody'.

So this insistence, this prescription ('keep truth and preference utterly separate, whatever the cost'), is what was both brave and heroic in the Enlightenment. When acted upon by brave people (think of Galileo or Darwin), it won important, indeed earth-shaking, truths for humanity out of the jaws of prejudice and dogma, often at considerable personal cost to the truth seekers involved.[7] Moreover, this prescription's importance and its heroism are shown by the fact that (unfortunately) a lot of people, even today, cannot live up to it in the 'crunch' cases where it matters—which means in the cases that matter to them. That is to say, many Christians and Moslems find it hard to consider the evidence for and against the existence of God dispassionately. A fair few of them find it hard to consider dispassionately the evidence for and against biological evolution.[8] Some feminists find it hard to consider dispassionately the evidence for and against the existence of biological differences between the sexes. A fair few environmentalists find it hard to weigh dispassionately the evidence for and against the desirability of natural scientific knowledge.

But if this insistence on 'dispassion at all costs and especially when it costs most' is what makes the Enlightenment so brave and heroic, it is also what makes it so dangerous. Because, as subsequent historical experience has shown, there is (contrary to the optimistic belief of most Enlightenment thinkers) no guar-antee that truths, once discovered, will always make humankind free, or even freer.[9] On the contrary, as we have insisted above, all truths can be politically or technologically used or abused in ways that are destructive and/or oppressive, not only of humankind itself, but of other life forms on this planet, and indeed of the planet itself. So this means, in effect, that truth may be pursued, courageously and in the face of greater or lesser opposition, 'for its own sake', only for such pursuit to result not in the greater happiness or wellbeing of humankind, but in its greater misery; not in an environmentally richer, healthier, more diverse planet, but in a global wasteland. The point here is that such a risk is not less 'just' because the truth is true, or because it has been pursued with whatever amount of courage, perseverance and intelligence. The pursuit and discovery of truth *may* be of benefit to human beings and the other plants and animals that inhabit this planet, but it may not. And in the twenty-first century (as against the eighteenth) all those who pursue truth must do so, and continue to do so in full awareness of that real risk and danger.

As we have seen, this is precisely the realisation used to justify postmodernist root-and-branch rejections of 'the Enlightenment project'. But such rejections typically involve a *de facto* denial of the heroism of the Enlightenment through a determined, but very uncourageous, avoidance of its dangers. Postmodernists not only fail to live up to the Enlightenment prescription to keep truth and preference distinct no matter what the cost, they make a positive political and philosophical virtue out of not doing so. They cop out of the dangers posed by pursuing truth 'for its own sake' (and in knowing, clear-eyed, disregard of all the possible nasty uses that may be made of it), by quite explicitly—not implicitly, or by default—equating truth with preference. The quotation from POLS/Fem 2 at the head of this chapter is a perfect example of a student doing precisely this.

However, and ironically, in this quotation the conception of truth that the author is critiquing is an explicitly relativistic one—i.e., it is Foucault's own conception. But this does not alter the fact that the 'grounds' on which s/he takes issue with it are not that such a position is philosophically unsustainable (i.e., itself untrue), but simply that it is inconvenient for, or destructive of, the feminist political project.

> If, as Foucault argues, knowledge is always produced and understood through power relations, and every account of the 'truth' is equal in its legitimacy, it seems impossible

for there to exist a collective authentic or coherent voice of 'woman' based in any group of women's experiences of the world.

To this student author, the question of whether Foucault's position even might be true is a non-issue. His position is 'seen as quite disturbing by many feminists' and 'serve(s) to legitimate the *status quo*', and these, apparently in themselves, are grounds enough to reject it.

Now, those of us who have little time for Foucault's view of the world might take some *Schadenfreude* pleasure in seeing his ideas critiqued using precisely the same 'political consequentialist' logic he routinely employed in critiquing the 'Enlightenment project' and a host of other things.[10] ('Those who live by consequentialist logic shall die by consequentialist logic' we might be tempted to reflect malevolently.)

But, however tempting it may be, we must eschew *Schadenfreude*, and require a critique of Foucault to meet precisely the same Enlightenment criteria of philosophical argumentation as any other critique of truth. So, to repeat, an 'Enlightenment' view of this matter would simply be:

Never mind whether Foucault's position is threatening to feminism, or supports the status quo, or even personally upsets you. *None* of that is the issue. The *only* issue is, *is it true or not*?

Needless to say, none of Bacon, Voltaire, Rousseau, Diderot or Hume, and still less Galileo, Darwin or Marx would have accepted an answer of the form, 'No, it is not true because it is threatening to feminism.' Nor would they would have accepted an answer of the form (strongly implied, at least, in the quotation), 'No, it is not true because a non-relativistic concept of truth is politically required to provide a "point" or "impetus" to feminism.'

Rather, they would all have required a demonstration that a relativistic conception of truth is not true and/or that a non-relativistic conception is true, and a demonstration that did not invoke, in any way, the consequences (political, social, cultural or personal) of its being held to be true. And note: they would demand such a demonstration, philosophically, even though each of them would, in fact, have rejected Foucault's relativism. Again, the central philosophical point is not that one rejects relativist or anti-relativist conceptions of truth, but the grounds on which one rejects them. (It is of course scarcely surprising that the student does not grasp this point, given that s/he is relying entirely on Foucault for his/her understanding of the Enlightenment!)

However this student author's political preference for a non-relativistic conception of truth is very unusual among students who endorse a postmodernist critique of the 'Enlightenment project'. It is much more common for them to prefer a relativistic conception. That is, it is much more common to find them arguing, as in the quotations from POLS/IR 10, that what is true varies between groups or cultures of human beings, so that what is true in and for one group or culture may not be true in and for another group or culture. This involves a point-blank denial of the Enlightenment's 'universalist' conception of truth, a denial usually expressed explicitly (as it is in the quotations from POLS/IR 10).

However, it turns out that this is, at bottom, just another way of equating truth with preference. For the postmodernist argument against universalism is, once again, not a philosophical argument at all, but an argument about the alleged nasty consequences of universalism—cultural imperialism, environmental destruction, etc. So, this more common postmodernist argument for relativism relies entirely on a consequentialist logic, just as much as the argument against relativism found in POLS/Fem 2. And, once again, the challenge and the danger of truth (and thus of the

Enlightenment) is evaded by that logic. And, once again, this comes at the cost of eviscerating the concept of truth of all meaning.

In their book *Intellectual Impostures*, Sokal and Bricmont provide a particularly revealing example of this. They report that a number of European anthropologists who have worked with the Zuni Native American people have found themselves in a difficult situation over the question of whether the ancestors of the Zuni and other Native American peoples came across the Bering Strait some 10–20,000 years ago (the standard archaeologically supported view), or whether, as Zuni and other Native American origin myths suggest, they have 'always' been in North America and sprang from a subterranean world of spirits. Sokal and Bricmont quote one of these anthropologists, a Dr Roger Anyon, as saying 'Science is just one of many ways of knowing the world . . . [The Zuni's world view is] just as valid as the archaeological viewpoint of what prehistory is about.' Sokal and Bricmont then comment:

Note first that the word 'valid' is ambiguous: is it intended in a cognitive sense, or in some other sense? If the latter, we have no objection, but the reference to 'knowing the world' suggests the former. Now, both in philosophy and in everyday language, there is a distinction between *knowledge* (understood, roughly, as justified true belief) and mere *belief*; that is why the word 'knowledge' has a positive connotation while 'belief' is neutral. What, then, does Anyon mean by 'knowing the world'? If he intends the word 'knowing' in its traditional sense, then his assertion is simply false: *the two theories in question are mutually incompatible, so they cannot both be true (or even approximately true).* If, on the other hand, he is simply noting that different people have different beliefs, then his assertion is true (and banal), but it is misleading to employ the success-word knowledge. [Emphasis added]

At the words 'approximately true', Sokal and Bricmont insert the following fascinating footnote:

> During a debate at New York University, where this example was mentioned, many people seemed not to understand or accept this elementary remark. The problem presumably comes, at least in part, from the fact that they have redefined 'truth' as a belief that is 'locally accepted as such' or else as an 'interpretation' that fulfils a given psychological and social role. It is difficult to say what shocks us the most: someone who believes that creation myths are true (in the usual sense of the word) or someone who adheres systematically to this redefinition of the word 'true'.[11]

Clearly what we have here is yet another example of the political and humanitarian support for a good cause leading to the utterly unnecessary adoption of bad philosophy. Aware of the suffering and oppression that Native American peoples have undergone at the hands of European conquerors, and of the way that oppression has been rationalised and justified by doctrines of cultural and intellectual superiority, sympathetic students of Native American society do not wish to be, or even perceived to be, continuing this awful history of cultural contempt. Hence they are unwilling to say that archaeological evidence conclusively shows certain creation myths to be false or untrue. So one of their number, employing a common tactic, uses the word 'valid' to show his respect for the myths while remaining neutral (let us say) about their truth.

But that is not the worst of it. For as Sokal and Bricmont's 'shocked' footnote about the NYU debate indicates, some people want to go further than this. They wish to say that it can be true *both* that Native American people came across the Bering Strait 10–20,000 years ago *and* that they have 'always' been in the Americas and (presumably) sprang from a subterranean world of spirits.

Now I share Sokal and Bricmont's shock, but I wish to go a little further than they did in commenting on this example. I want to make clear some of the intellectual and political implications of holding the conviction that both these propositions can be true simultaneously (because one is 'true' in western culture and the other is 'true' in Native American culture). I want to do this because I think that neither the well-intentioned students in the NYU debate, nor many of the similarly well-intentioned Australian honours students I have taught and supervised, really comprehend what such views commit them to philosophically and politically. And I think *they* would be shocked if they did!

If the above cultural relativist proposition is true then, logically, the following must also be true.

1. Only 'outsider' anthropologists can understand and endorse the archaeological evidence that supports the Bering migration, no Native American person can, because:

2. if any Native American person did understand and endorse such evidence they would cease (culturally) to be a Native American person, because

3. if a Native American person did understand and endorse the archaeological evidence then they would (presumably) cease to believe that the creation myths were true. But,

4. you can't cease to believe in the truth of the creation myths and still be a 'real' or 'true' Native American person.

In other words, and just as a matter of logic, you can *only* believe that it is 'true' for westerners that the ancestors of Native Americans came across the Bering Strait and 'true' for Zuni and other peoples that they didn't, by embracing a form of 'identity essentialism' which I think can properly be called racist. Because if truth is *not* evidentially supported belief, but a matter of cultural identity, then no one can change their views about what is true without changing their culture. That is, a Zuni person who says 'I used to think that we had always been here, but now I know we came across the Bering Strait' ceases to be Zuni. And a westerner who says 'I used to think that the Zuni people came across the Bering Strait, but now I know that they were always in North America' ceases to be a westerner.

But this is nonsense. Zuni people can learn to understand archaeological evidence, can conclude on the basis of such evidence that their origin myths may not be literally true, but still endorse such myths as identity-defining, beautiful, valuable in instructing the young, and so forth. And of course some Zuni people have done so. Most importantly of all, any and all Zuni people can do all this without ceasing to be Zuni.

And in the case of westerners, the Sokal and Bricmont quotation shows that while 'western' anthropologists and archaeologists cannot accept the Zuni origin myths as true, because they are not true, they can still treat them with respect and admiration, and appreciate their social and aesthetic role in Zuni culture. They can abandon western cultural imperialism and contempt toward Native American peoples without ceasing to be westerners.

And both these things can happen because all human cultures are dynamic, changing, flexible *contexts* in which people live their lives. They are not essentialist, historically static prisons.

In short, then, an extreme cultural relativism about truth, which begins as an admirable attempt to treat other cultures—particularly cultures that have been the object of western contempt and oppression—with the respect they are due, ironically ends up endorsing an almost racist essentialism about culture. Perhaps most importantly of all, abandoning a universalist conception of truth (as evidentially justified belief) in order to accommodate and respect cultural difference ends by contemptuously patronising those cultures and their peoples. It does so by saying, in effect, 'Truth may be evidentially justified belief *to us*, but obviously it is quite something else *to you*, and we think that "something else" is equally "valid".'

But truth is evidentially justified belief for *everybody*, whether Zuni, Iroquois, Australian Aboriginal, Hindu, Buddhist, Moslem, Christian, whatever. It is just that what is accepted as evidence may vary from culture to culture, and even in the same culture through time. But that this is so means that any and all people can change their views on what should count as evidence and on why different types of evidence are, or are not, compelling, without in any way endangering their identities (cultural or otherwise). Indeed such changes of view are historically commonplace, historically normal, in all human cultures—western and non-western.

So, to conclude, postmodernists (including my student authors) have been right—though not original—in observing that the eighteenth-century Enlightenment thinkers were far too optimistic in believing that the unswerving pursuit of truth through the application of reason would always be positive or liberating for humankind (let alone for their fellow creatures or for the planet on which they live). Two hundred years of deeply ambiguous history since the Enlightenment should have left no one in any doubt about this.

Postmodernists are profoundly wrong, however, in thinking that the correct response to this history lesson is a radical redefinition of the concept of truth—so that what is 'true' is what some group of human beings find 'right' or 'good', or so that what truth is varies from culture to culture.

They are wrong for several reasons. First, that one should only believe what is true is a universal human belief, so debating what is true is something that every human being can do with every other human being. Such debates may not result in agreement (especially if there are crucial cultural, religious or other derived differences about what is and is not acceptable evidence), but they can result in enhanced mutual understanding. They can do this, however, only because all human beings believe that a proposition is true if there is evidence to support it. That is to say, no human beings believe that a proposition is true just because they would prefer it to be, or just because life would be better if it were, or just because it is culturally important to them that it should be. And that is why all human beings can debate about truth.[12]

Second, the 'Enlightenment project' was, and still remains, an enormously courageous and dangerous (courageous because dangerous) project. Essentially its courage consists in taking the risk that, if truth is pursued and discovered (irrespective of cost and irrespective of consequences), human beings will find a way to deal productively with whatever that truth turns out to be.[13] And, to repeat myself again, this is dangerous because that belief may itself not be true! It may therefore be that Enlightenment courage will turn out to have been misplaced, and the risk of pursuing truth turn out not to have been worth taking—perhaps even turn out to have catastrophic consequences.[14] But, third, if that is so, it will not be because of the truths themselves (whatever they are), but because human beings do not have the wisdom, or compassion, or sophistication, to deal with those truths in a productive way—for each other, for other forms of life on the planet, or for the planet itself. Fourth, this just means that what really determines, and will determine, whether the 'Enlightenment project' risk was worth taking is not the process itself of truth discovery, but what human beings do—politically, socially, interculturally, environmentally—with the truths they discover. It therefore follows that it is not only philosophically incoherent, and politically very dangerous, to abandon the 'Enlightenment project' (by eviscerating the concept of truth), it is completely *unnecessary*, even if the 'project's' legacy over the past 200 or so years is distinctly ambiguous. All that is necessary is to join the political struggles to make that legacy positive or productive rather than destructive, in whatever area or dimension of life.

I do not believe that any of the student authors with whose work I have been concerned in this book have actually thought through the philosophical implications of equating truth with preference, or that they actually intended to argue seriously for such an equation. If they had, they would soon have discovered the obvious contradictions that I have drawn out in this chapter. Rather, they are just so appalled at some of the things that have been done in the name of 'truth' and 'enlightenment' over the past two centuries that, in effect, they have been led down the path to philosophical incoherence by righteous indignation. Indeed, as must by now be obvious, this chapter really represents a further, and deeper, exploration of the way pursuing good causes can lead to bad philosophy—the issue with which I was concerned in Chapter 9.

I hope, therefore, I have shown that in the case of the Enlightenment, just as in the cases dealt with in Chapter 9, it is not politically desirable to do bad philosophy in support of good causes. Those good causes can be far better pursued through doing good philosophy and (more importantly) by bringing to them a good heart, clear political goals based on detailed empirical knowledge of the world, and the courageous determination in pursuit of those goals so perfectly exemplified by the great Enlightenment thinkers.

11. Tips for teachers and supervisors

In common with many of my colleagues I hold that the primary protocol of anyone acting as a dissertation supervisor in the social sciences and humanities must be that a student is entitled to write the thesis that s/he wishes to write.

In the context of this book, the implication of accepting that protocol is, of course, that if a student wishes to write a thesis making use of a Foucauldian, or poststructuralist, or postmodernist theoretical perspective they are perfectly entitled to do so. Therefore, the role of their supervisor must be restricted to ensuring that they do so in the best possible way, not to directly challenging their choice of theoretical perspective.

Some of my colleagues take the view that if they are totally unsympathetic to the theoretical perspective a student wishes to adopt they can, and should, refuse to supervise the student, but recommend them to a colleague whom they know would be more sympathetic. I cannot concur with this view or practice, mainly because I think it constitutes a *de facto* infraction of the protocol above, but in any case it can be an unaffordable luxury in small academic departments where the range of supervisory expertise is limited. In such departments one will, at least occasionally, find oneself required to supervise dissertations about which one is profoundly sceptical. The question therefore arises as to what one should do in those cases.

I think a good general guide here can be found in Walter Bagehot's famous discussion of the three rights of a monarch in a constitutional monarchy—'the right to be consulted, the right to encourage, the right to warn'.[1] A supervisor has a right to be consulted in detail about what a student intends to do in their thesis, s/he has a right to encourage them to do it in a way which is, in the supervisor's view, the best possible way within the theoretical framework chosen, and s/he has a right to warn them of difficulties that they may encounter on examination if certain weaknesses (theoretical or empirical) in the thesis are not addressed. However, if having received both encouragement and warning the student decides to proceed in ways which the supervisor still thinks profoundly problematic, the supervisor has (in my view, at least) no right to prevent them doing so, nor do they have the right to withdraw, or threaten to withdraw, their supervision as a means of changing a student's approach.

The kind of dissertations reviewed in this book, however, offer very specific problems for supervisors deriving from the fact that the 'theoretical' approach involved raises a number of profound philosophical issues, issues a teacher in Political Science, Sociology or Cultural Studies may not even recognise, let alone be equipped to deal with, and issues that are profoundly contentious even among professional philosophers. (Referring the student to a philosopher colleague or inviting a professional philosopher to act as co-supervisor may not resolve these issues.) In fact, one of my aims in writing this book has been to alert my colleagues to these oft-unrecognised philosophical issues in postmodernist theory, and to provide some indication of their depth and difficulty.

However, although understanding—knowing how to recognise—these problems is a necessary starting point in improving supervision of these types of theses, such understanding does not, in and of itself, tell one how best to deal with them—that is, how best to advise students so that such problems are minimised or eliminated.

Therefore, I provide below some general tips on supervisory techniques that may help in this regard. Since I have identified the problems in postmodernist theory as deriving primarily from certain uses of language—uses which seem 'innocent', but which have, in fact, certain inbuilt deep philosophical difficulties—then all the tips concern language use. They involve encouraging students to use certain linguistic formulations and to avoid others, and warning them of the kind of philosophical and logical issues that may emerge if they choose not to take this advice.

Here, then, are the tips:

(1) *In the theoretical chapters or parts of the thesis, discourage the widespread or frequently repeated use of sentences that place abstractions in subject positions.* That is, a kind of permanent supervisory scepticism about sentences beginning 'This theoretical perspective ensures . . .' or 'This approach encourages . . .' or 'Subjectivities are constructed by . . .' or 'The matrix of power produces . . .' is very useful. This scepticism should have as much to do with the frequency as the presence of such sentences. Occasional uses of such formulations are harmless enough, and indeed normal in virtually all intellectual work.[2] Their *dense* use, however, especially when a student is self-consciously theorising, betrays the presence of a mind-set which has lost, or is losing, all sense of human agency. Pointing out to the student that these formulations may be replaced by explicitly peopled synonyms (or at least enquiring as to whether they might be/could be) can be a way of indirectly challenging that mind-set (and perhaps be more effective than a direct challenge).

(2) *Be conscious of both the reificatory and redundancy implications*
    of certain kinds of much-favoured 'theoretical' nouns and noun
    phrases. Thus, if a student writes 'ideational structures' where
    they could simply say 'ideas', or speaks of something 'having'
    'forms of meaning' when they could simply say that X *means*
    something, or speaks of something as an 'example' or 'case' of
    'power relations' where they simply mean that X has power
    over Y, or X dominates Y, or (even) X influences Y, draw these
    uses of language to their attention, and at least ask whether
    they are necessary or if they could be replaced by less reifying
    synonyms. In this context, it is especially important to be
    aware that, in English at least, it is almost always possible
    to replace active forms of the verb by passive forms, and to
    turn verbs into nouns or noun phrases. By this I mean that
    it is always possible to render, say, 'Stories in the mass media
    frequently suggested that no one could seriously believe . . .'
    as 'Certain beliefs were constructed by mass media discourse
    to appear as non-entities—as nullities or impossibilities—in
    audience conceptions.' The point about this latter rendition
    is not merely that it is wordy and pretentious (although it is),
    but that turning a repeated action or practice ('frequently
    suggesting' that some belief or view is implausible or false)
    into quasi- or conceptual things ('non-entities', 'nullities'
    or 'impossibilities')[3] creates that theoretical world or land-
    scape of abstract 'objects' whose intellectually damaging
    consequences I have analysed at length in this book. In fact,
    supervisors should note that

(3) *using linguistic forms which turn repeated or habitual human*
    acts into quasi-things—'discourse', 'structures of meaning',
    'power', 'belief structures', 'relations of . . .' *is the most common*
    technique employed in creating the world of theory.[4] Almost
    invariably, it is followed by the endowing of these quasi-things
    with attributes or powers of their own. Therefore pointing

out to students that there are nearly always alternative ways of speaking of habitual or institutionalised actions or practices—ways which do not turn them into quasi-things— has two advantages. First, it raises the question of whether theoretical entities are 'just' ways of speaking or writing about repeated human actions or practices. Second, and less obviously, it also raises the question of why we speak in these reificatory ways, and of what we mean to say when we do. That is, it raises the question of whether what we have here are 'just metaphors' or 'names of real things'—the question I suggested in Chapter 1 is so important to raise, but so seldom raised in postmodernist theory. And if one answer to that question is that such reificatory words and phrases are treated as metaphors in ordinary use, but are taken much more ontologically seriously in 'theory', then the student will at least need to reflect on this discrepancy and what it might mean for theory and theorising. I should add here that supervisors should also

(4) *discourage students from turning what are often (i.e., in many empirical contexts) perfectly compatible methodological approaches into abstract things by adding '-ism' ('constructivism', 'positivism', 'empiricism', 'structuralism', 'poststructuralism', etc.).* This kind of theoretical reification can be very distorting of students' study practices because such a use of 'isms' creates another reified world of apparently discrete 'things' (in this case philosophical and methodological 'things') out of what may be, in fact, perfectly compatible approaches to a given subject of study. If they are presented and conceived as discrete, and indeed incompatible, 'things' or 'entities', students may feel constrained to choose among or between them, when no exclusive choice is necessary and when mixing approaches may be the best means of doing good empirical work.

(5) *Strongly discourage all talk and writing about 'language' as an entity, and especially such writing as makes 'language' an active subject and has it 'constructing' or 'determining' this, that, or the other.* Here it is appropriate to point out that this is an approach to language and meaning that was radically criticised 70 years ago. Therefore one can, at the very least, suggest to students that they learn something about this critique and what its implications might be for their work. However it is equally vital for supervisors to

(6) *stress to students that abandoning the notion that 'language' is an entity that can 'do' anything, does not involve abandoning the notion that certain **uses** of language can be constraining of the thoughts and activities of people, up to and including their ideas about who and what they are—their identities or subjectivities.* For while 'language' does not prevent anybody thinking or saying anything, it does not follow from this that particular people in particular places at particular times can say, or think, anything that they want to say or think. It may be that they cannot, but why they cannot needs to be investigated in each particular case. Such an investigation may certainly use as a testing hypothesis the idea that they do not have the forms of language necessary either to say—or even to conceive—what they might want to say, or would benefit from being able to say or conceive. What it must not do, however, is assume that the problem is linguistic, when this may be only one possibility, only one possible explanation. In short, it is important to stress to students that what linguistic constructivism or discourse constructivism says is not simply false. Rather, it deterministically overgeneralises an important but specific (empirically specific) insight. This generally means that

(7) *supervisors can assure students that they can say anything and everything political or ethical that they wish to say about any*

(empirical) issue without using either 'discourse theory' or 'social constructivism'. This is just another way of saying what I have suggested at length in the book—that advocating good political causes does not require the use of bad philosophy. Since for many students the cause is what matters most, this assurance can often be very effective in getting them to change approach.

12. Conclusions

This book has as its motto a quotation from Wittgenstein stating that the task of philosophy is to unravel knots in thinking, and I have rather self-consciously pursued this analogy through a number of its chapters. But of course the unravelling of knots is a rather negative business. S/he who ties a knot in a piece of string or rope at least creates something, but when the knots are unravelled, all that is left is the string or rope as it was before it became knotted. Indeed, the clear implication of Wittgenstein's analogy is that when the 'knots in our thinking' have been unravelled, what will remain will be rather obvious, even banal. Elsewhere in his work he says that, although his philosophy is destructive, all it destroys is 'houses of cards', or 'castles in the air'. Such destruction may give the sufferer from philosophical delusion some intellectual and psychological relief but it changes nothing in the world beyond that.[1]

And all that certainly fits with what I think I have done in this book. For, at its end, what can we say? We can say that:

- people use language, language does not use people, therefore
- if there are things wrong with the world—if there is injustice, discrimination, oppression—that is

because of what people do (or omit to do) not because of what language does (or omits to do). Of course, it is true that

- in being unjust, in discriminating unfairly against others, in oppressing other peoples or other cultures, people may use language in ways that are stereotyping or demeaning, and in ways that justify, or disguise, their unjust or discriminatory behaviour (by 'disguise' here we may mean from themselves as well as from others). Also

- if those who are treated unjustly or oppressively, or who are demeaned by those more powerful than themselves, accept or internalise the language that explains or justifies that state of affairs, such internalisation may weaken their sense of self-worth and dignity, even crucially affect their sense of identity. But, even so,

- in *both* these cases we are dealing with human vices, nastinesses, weaknesses and frailties and the way in which these are 'expressed' in language. We are not dealing with anything that 'language' (as a curious subject) does. And that this is so is shown clearly by the fact that,

- the same language (or natural languages) that can be used to oppress, bully and demean, can also be used to resist oppression, rally the bullied and build self-confidence and self-belief among those who have been demeaned. Of course language will only be used to liberate others, or oneself, if there are people around who want to do either or both of these things. But, equally,

- language will only be used to oppress, bully and demean, if there are people around who want to do that, or whose interest lies in doing that. And none of this is the less true because,

■ people may be genuinely convinced that their unjust behaviour is not so, or that their discrimination against others is justified in some way or other, or that (say) their own oppression is a 'natural' or 'unchangeable' state of affairs about which they can and should do nothing—and may *use* language to express all these convictions. For,

■ if any or all of these convictions are unjustified or false, or have terrible social or political consequences, then the blame for that lies with the people (including the oppressed or demeaned) who use language in these ways, not in the language that they use. 'The fault, dear Brutus, lies in ourselves, and not in our language, that we are underlings.' This is not to deny that,

■ the use of power by the powerful to terrorise and oppress, and/or the lack of self-confidence or self-belief among the oppressed may make resistance (let alone revolt or revolution) difficult or impossible in some/many cases. But if this is the case then (and to repeat once more),

■ it is so because of the power and powerlessness of people (in which their use of language may play a role) not because of the power of language (or 'discourse') as such.

I think it would be right to call all the above observations 'banalities', statements of the obvious, recapitulations of what we 'all' know. They are as banal, as 'straightforward', in fact, as a piece of string once its knots have been untied.

But equally, or so it appears from the student theses anyway, none of these observations are at all 'obvious' while there are theoretical knots in the understanding. Which is as much as to say that the kind of theory I have been dealing with in this book actively prevents students seeing what they could perfectly easily have seen before they started using it. More than that, it also involves them in explicitly or implicitly denying what they would never have dreamed of denying before they started using it. I cannot imagine a more appropriate specification of what my cavalier phrase 'wasting their time and addling their brains' might mean.

But in saying this I must myself be wary of self-contradiction. For am I now not saying that some piece or form of language (the piece or form called 'theory') *is* actively preventing students from seeing the obvious, even actively causing them to deny the obvious? And if that's what I'm saying, am I not contradicting my own thesis? For this certainly sounds as if 'language' is doing, even causing, something.

But no, I am not saying that. I am saying that it is the students 'as people' who used theoretical language in ways that allowed them to obscure or deny things they wanted to obscure or deny. But if I want to say that, I have to come up with a reason why they might want to do such an odd thing.

Here is one such reason. From the 1980s to the present our world has not been a good one to inhabit for people of a left-wing or even a left-liberal persuasion. This period has seen, among other things:

- the discrediting of the practice, and much of the theory of 'actually existing socialism' in the wake of the collapse of the USSR;
- the triumph of neo-liberal or 'free market' economic policy-making in nearly all states of the world (including former communist states) and at the global level;

- the retreat, in the face of this triumph, of even 'gradualist' forms of social democracy and welfare state, especially in Western Europe (their previous heartland);

- the waning of the influence of feminism among younger generations of women, even, and in fact especially, among those women who have been the principle 'objective' beneficiaries of the changes and reforms for which feminists fought; and

- the tendency of 'the Left' in the face of all this to disintegrate into a variety of 'specific issue' pressure groups and campaigns, with the result that, even where such groups make significant advances (say in regard to environmental issues or particular 'human rights' campaigns), there is no expectation that these advances will have any broader consequences or resonance.

In fact, the most pronounced single effect of all these changes has been to further reinforce the tendency of left-leaning people to see themselves as engaged in 'resistance' (significantly a quite popular word with several of the sample authors) to what is, rather than an active struggle to change anything. Indeed historical periods such as the one through which we are now living tend to be marked by the strong presence of 'radical pessimism' among those on the Left—i.e., a tendency to see politics as a possibly vain but necessary struggle to stop things getting even worse, rather than as a means of making things better.

In such a situation, it is difficult for any thinking person not to ask the question, why has all this happened? And it is especially difficult to resist the question as to why all or the majority of people affected by the changes itemised not only acquiesced in, but actually supported them.

Now one answer to this threatening question (and one that has a long history on the Left) is that in so far as it is a product of popular ignorance, or of some kind of popular failure to perceive reality and/or to understand it aright, such support is not real or genuine. And clearly if peoples' main tool for understanding the world—their use of language—can be shown to have been 'distorted', or 'manipulated', or subtly undermined in some way (so that its application yields false results, or is even self-destructive for the people using it) then one can come up with an analytical outcome that is at least psychologically comforting. That is, 'reactionary' policies and tendencies may have popular support, but this support is not 'real' because it is not, in fact, an outcome of the application of rational judgement. Rather it is the product of either elite manipulation of language or of the 'distorting' power of 'language' or 'discourse' affecting both rulers and ruled, elites and masses. And it also follows from this analysis that if the power of 'language' or 'discourse' can itself be challenged or undermined, then the scales will fall from the eyes of all, and the door swing open to better, more 'progressive' policies and futures.

In short then, bad times for the Left are perfect times for left-wing theories of 'ideology' by which the badness of those times can be both affirmed politically and denied psychologically. They are affirmed politically in that their badness is stated, and indeed emphasised. But they are denied psychologically in that a version of the bad is painted in which the vast majority of people are simply its victims, rather than its perpetrators.[2]

In this context, then, theories of the power of language or discourse are just the latest in a long line of Left theories of 'false consciousness', which have been around since the late nineteenth century when Engels (not Marx) coined the phrase,[3] and which have always fulfilled this particular dual function. Such theories always combine deterministic gloom (nothing can change as long as the power of 'language', 'discourse' or 'ideology' rules) with almost millenarian hope (but everything can change once 'language', 'discourse' or 'ideology' are changed) in one deeply satisfying psychological brew.[4] Since, of course, intellectuals (and for this purpose we will class students as intellectuals) deal almost entirely in words—in language—then it is not overly difficult to persuade them, or rather for them to persuade themselves, that changing language, in and of itself, can have momentous consequences, even though (or perhaps because) it is so difficult to do!

I need hardly add that I don't think any of this is true. That is, I do not think it is necessary to invoke the power of language or discourse or ideology to explain any of the setbacks suffered by Left politics in the last 30 years, nor is it necessary to invoke them to explain mass popular support for, or acquiescence in, those changes. This is not the place for me to say what my preferred explanations of these phenomena would be, but suffice it to say that none of them involve postulating that—for example—support for neo-liberal policies, or waning enthusiasm for certain aspects of welfare states, or increasing caution among many women about identifying as feminists is *eo ipso* 'irrational'. In all these cases, however, it is possible to argue that the popular responses involved occur for fairly mundane, straightforward reasons without their longer-term or broader social consequences being fully realised.

At any rate, this is not the issue here. The issue is, we may remember, to explain why a significant number of intelligent students might be brought to embrace the extraordinary proposition that language uses people, in place of the more obvious (and true) observation that people use language. The broad 'sociology of knowledge' explanation I have given above is, I am sure, sound. It postulates the appearance (or rather reappearance, for the umpteenth time) of a deterministic leftist

Weltanschauung (a self-protective *Weltanschauung*) that students just 'pick up' from some of their teachers and from their reading, and reproduce.

However, there may also be another, much narrower, explanation working mainly in tandem with the broader socio-logical one above, but also—very occasionally—on its own, to produce the same result—the embrace of this extraordinary linguistically determinist world view. And if this narrower explanation is also correct, it will constitute a final, crowning irony with which to end this book. Because it is possible I think that the linguistic determinism of the kind of postmodernist or poststructuralist theory I have outlined in this book is true (i.e., empirically true) in one case—*itself*!

For it seems to me at least possible that if students use language in the kind of syntactically-tortured, abstraction-loaded, metaphorically impersonal ways which we have reviewed in detail in this book, then language may indeed end up using them—by which I mean that they may end up quite simply not knowing what they are saying! More specifically, the students in question may end up (and I think I have shown that they have ended up) not understanding even the more obvious implications of what they are saying—whether these implications be logical or political.

Another way of putting this might be to say that if you abuse language 'it' will abuse you. For this to occur, however, the form of abuse involved has to be rather peculiar and specific. It has to be a form of abuse of language not recognised as such by those practising it.

In this book I have suggested that the way this happens among the student authors surveyed is through their initial act of creating a 'theoretical' landscape or space—a landscape or space they then fill with a range of abstract, conceptual 'objects'—among which language itself is both the most notable and the most fatal. I have suggested that it is the intellectual moment that the students think of as both foundational and clarifying—the 'theoretical' moment itself, the moment when they *start* doing theory—which is actually the moment of their deepest confusion, the moment when they most deeply abuse their own language. For though they may, thereafter, go on to reason very logically from the abstract premises they have created, if those premises are confused then the conclusions from such reasoning will be equally confused. Moreover, those same deeply confused 'objectivist' premises will simultaneously distort any empirical research the students may undertake, or generalise from, using those premises.

So it may be, to repeat, that the propositions 'language uses people', 'language abuses people', 'language distorts thinking' are true, but only of and in this kind of theory! For in the vast range of normal, everyday uses of language (including those found, for example, in science and engineering laboratories) the clarity, if not the truth, of what is said is more or less guaranteed by the context of other practices and actions within which that use occurs, or which it accompanies. But the kind of 'theoretical practice' we are reviewing here is precisely a practice with words, and only with words, a practice largely 'undisciplined' by any broader, non-linguistic 'action' context, and this makes it very vulnerable to the kind of utterly unintended, but 'deep' abuse, described in this book.

To be fair, this kind of postmodernist or poststructuralist theory is not absolutely unique as a case of such deep, but utterly unintended, abuse of language. For if Wittgenstein's later philosophy is right, then philosophy itself, or at least a very great deal of it, is another such case. Indeed Wittgenstein is famous for having argued that 'there are no philosophical problems', by which he meant that all the examples of such 'problems' (the 'problem of induction', the 'problem of knowledge of the external world', the 'problem of solipsism', etc.) are artefacts of philosophers' own deep abuse of language. They are produced by the way that philosophers themselves linguistically set up these 'problems', with each set-up involving an utterly unintended and 'deep' abuse of language. Thus diagnose and unravel the abuse in each set-up, and the problem disappears or is 'dissolved'.[5]

This is not the place to consider the merits of Wittgenstein's deeply contentious arguments about philosophy. (Although the close parallel with the issue of theoretical 'set-up' which I have diagnosed in this book should be obvious, as should the significance of my earlier characterisation of theory as 'abortive semi-philosophy'—it is possible that these two anomalous cases are just two variants of one case.) What I do wish to emphasise, however, is that even if it is true that language can use people in this kind of theory and/or in philosophy, we must be clear as to precisely what is true, even in these cases.

Four paragraphs ago I made the dangerously pithy but pleasingly pugnacious observation that 'if you abuse language "it" will abuse you'. This observation is, I think, true. But another way of putting that truth is to use reflexive forms of the verb, i.e., 'you abuse yourself by abusing your language' or, even better, 'you abuse your own intelligence by abusing your language'. These reflexive forms are the better ways in which to put it. For even in the case of the very odd 'theoretical' and 'philosophical' abuses of language we have been considering in this book, it is people who are doing the abusing, not language. I think it is true to say that many of the student authors who are the subject of this book have, albeit unintentionally, abused their own intelligence in writing their theses. But to repeat for one last time, their language itself did nothing. For language, not being a 'thing', can no more be a subject than it can be an object. That is, language does nothing, nor is anything done to it, although particular parts of language may be used by people to do things to themselves, to others, to the world around them.

Finally: that we live in a time when many intelligent and idealistic young people need to redescribe confronting facts about the world just to make them bearable; that we live in a time when faith in the Enlightenment project has been lost, and its passionately courageous universalism diluted to a safe, pallid, cringing relativism; that we live in a time when excellent students are encouraged to take flight into the obscurantism of 'theory' rather than use their abilities to investigate the world and to say clearly, even pugnaciously, what they want to say—all this strikes me, and indeed many other people, as deeply sad.

But times change. We cannot say that we have been here before, for though cyclical history never simply repeats itself. Certainly there have been other times in history when those who defined themselves as 'on the Left' faced a bleak outlook. Those times, however, did not last, in part because the very marginalisation and weakening of 'Left' values and practices that produces such gloom, also has very damaging implications for millions and even billions of 'non-Left' people. And so, for that reason alone, the pendulum tends to swing. Left-wing views and voices begin to be listened to again, become influential again.

But of course there is nothing automatic or *mechanically* self-correcting about this process. On the contrary, it has only ever occurred because, in the midst of the dark times, left-wing thought and politics were renewed, with such renewals being based precisely on facing harsh realities head-on and finding new policies and new approaches (but based on the same fundamental values) to meet them. Finding such policies and approaches is part of the way in which a wider world is convinced that there *are* alternatives to 'right-wing' or 'conservative' policies, that such ways are both practical and worth supporting, and that, therefore, the pendulum should be given a push leftwards.

So, bad times are good times for hard work. But bad times are also the worst times for flights into denial or wishful thinking (however tempting they may make them). By taking such flights—in effect, running away—one is only contributing one's halfpennyworth to *keeping* the bad times rolling. And surely even 'theorists' don't want that!

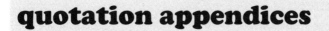

quotation appendices

In the appendices, comments by the author appear
within square brackets in quoted material,
and in **bold** before or after quoted material.

Appendix 1:
Doing theory

1.1 Through this explanation it becomes clear how constructivist theory can account for the collapse of the Soviet Union and not be forced to reduce it to a unique phenomenon that occurred within the international system due to theoretical constraints. The theoretical framework of constructivism has made provisions for such a transformation, realism relies on the perpetuation of the current order in an attempt to explain change.

POLS/IR 1 p. 19

1.2 While an epistemic communities approach to understanding international environmental agreements is an important step, on closer examination it can be seen that this theory also simplifies how agreement is reached in environmental diplomacy. The problem . . . lies in the fact that this theory removes science from politics as it describes a unidirectional flow of knowledge from scientific experts to the policy making community, who then implement [*sic*] this unified knowledge. This theory fails to see the important role that language plays in interpreting information and persuading audiences at every level of the research and policy making process . . .

POLS/IR 8 pp. 13–14

1.3 I do not contend that Chinese culture cannot think causally, nor that Australia cannot think in terms of 'tendency'. Notions of 'causality' and 'tendency' reveal different philosophical traditions which have necessarily influenced Australian and Chinese culture by their very existence.

POLS/IR 9 pp. 19–20

1.4 This metaphysic centres on 'the basic conviction that there must be some permanent, ahistorical matrix or framework to which we can ultimately appeal in determining the nature of rationality, truth, reality, goodness or rightness' [inset quote is from Bernstein's *Beyond Objectivism and Relativism,* p. 8]. This framework presumes that explanations will be true to the extent that they accurately reflect empirical reality, to the extent that they correspond to the facts.

1.5 The space of 'nomad thought' is qualitatively different from state space. State space is striated or grided [*sic*], regimented and controlled. Nomad space is open and smooth. We can see again in this image Deleuze and Guattari's critique of dominant forms (state forms) of discourse and their attempt to open up the space of theory in a way that avoids the process of model building. Avoiding [*sic*] the totalising and universal ways of the realist enlightenment philosophies of liberalism and marxism.

1.6 It is the role of institutions such as the discipline of IR and other state philosophies to act as a recoding mechanism for these decoded flows. International relations theory functions to create a separate political domain, 'abstract machine' or subsystem, apart from society. It provides a separate representational space, by its own procedural rules, with its own perceptual apparatuses and forms of expression. It is a process of transformation, completely at home among bodies whose movement it translates. It transposes movements into its particular arena and then retransmits them, in modified form. It is a 'force converter' as opposed to a categorical model. It gathers up movements of desire, rephrases them, then changes their direction, sending them back to propagate at ground-level in waves of ordering. It is not moral, just managerial.

What it demands of its subjects is a practical acceptance of certain parameters of action, rather than a purblind conformity to an absolute ideal.

POLS/IR 10 pp. 9, 50–1 and 69–70

1.7 For Foucault, power and knowledge are inherently connected and form an extremely important basis for his analysis of power. Foucault sees that there 'are to be found a whole domain of knowledge [*sic*], a whole type of power' [quote from *Discipline and Punish*, p. 185]. Where one concept is present, so is the other. Jon Simmons furthers this explanation, arguing that for Foucault 'Power/knowledge is a knot that is not meant to be unravelled' [J. Simmons, *Foucault and the Political*, London: Routledge, 1995, p. 27]. The correlation and co-dependency of these two concepts goes further, meaning that one cannot be understood or analysed without the other. Simmons explains that both knowledge and power relationships constitute one another because it is through an analysis of this relationship that our social world becomes knowable and therefore governable.

1.8 If the collection of knowledge, data and statistics can determine a power relationship, then the withholding of that knowledge must also have a part to play in unequal power structures and relationships. My argument is that, for example, the very existence of detention centres and the manner in which they are run and presented to the public, limits the amount of knowledge Australian citizens have about detainees. This therefore limits the power that Australian citizens can have in relation to those in detention. Foucault explains this as 'modifying the field of information' which in turn can 'produce effects of power'. The prison has become an important and permanent structure in our societies and the way that punishment is used to control 'criminals' is mirrored in the ways that society is controlled by those mechanisms of power. Society not only becomes involved in the power to punish, but prisons have also come to represent a discourse of power above as well as within the social body. Prisons and punishment structures have become a spectacle and performance of power for the government. At the same time those state structures have been able to maintain a level of secrecy and private knowledge.

POLS/IR 15 pp. 11 and 12, 29–30

1.9 . . . the poststructuralist approach . . . suggests that security is a practice: a political technology that facilitates the drawing together of sovereignty and identity . . . Security utilises the classical conception of sovereignty as an explanation for the nature of state actions and the dynamics of the international system. Simultaneously, security deploys a discourse of identity that connects individual subjectivity with broader sentiments of belonging. Combining these appeals to sovereignty and identity under the rubric of 'security' facilitates the construction of an intricate network of power relations and meaning. Central to this discourse is the notion that the external 'other' presents a threat not only to a state's territory, but to its collective identity.

Conversely, the 'individualising techniques' [*sic*] envisaged by Foucault centres on the concept of discipline and relies on forms of self-regulation to create productive citizens who are closely connected to wider state formations.

POLS/IR 16 pp. 15 and 16

1.10 By demonstrating how power relations function in the construction of truth, Foucault seeks to create space for the articulation of new knowledges, new truths. Thus whilst discourse is always an 'instrument and effect of power', acknowledging the relationship between truth and power ensures discourses' potential to be 'a hindrance, a stumbling block, a point of resistance and a starting point of an opposing strategy' is also recognised. Foucault wants society to realise its potential for resistance and transformation.

POLS/IR 18 p. 36

1.11 His later understanding of power in *Power/Knowledge, The History of Sexuality Volume 1* and 'The Subject and Power' puts forward 'an agonistic model of power'—'a set of actions upon other actions' in which 'discourse transmits and produces power; it reinforces it, but also undermines and exposes it, renders it fragile and makes it possible to thwart it'. Resistance to power is the assertion of 'truth' that is also constituted by discourses, whether 'reverse discourses' or 'counter discourses' to the dominant discourse. He claims that in order for a relationship of power to exist, a subject must be capable of action or resistance and be recognised as a person on whom power is exercised.

1.12 . . . Foucault asserts that 'individuals continuously contest fixed identities and relations in subtle ways' [quotation from Foucault, *Power/Knowledge: Selected Interviews and other Writings 1972–77*]. That is, power through domination produces greater possibilities for resistance by subjects. However, if the possibilities for resisting power are contained within power itself, then where are the sites for resisting it located?

1.13 Women's identities can develop through local and specific sites of resistance in the politics of difference, but no particular identity is more foundational or essential than others.

[Foucault's] analysis of discourse opens up an understanding of the nature and location of power within different discursive regimes. This has allowed postmodern feminists to locate and establish alternate knowledge bases for the legitimacy of women, in view of different ethnic, class and sexual backgrounds.

Foucault says that identity is produced through variable forces and discursive fields. Butler takes this one step further by claiming that, given that identity is an affect of power relations, it cannot be taken uncritically as the foundation on which on which, for example, feminists theorises [*sic*] and propose strategies for political ends for 'women' . . . Coalitional politics which emphasises unity, like the theories of Bordo and Grosz, privilege unity over the fragmentation and conflict that may need to be recognised and left unresolved for a truer appreciation of the multiple identities of 'women' if that label can still be used.

POLS/Fem 2 pp. 15, 16, 18–19 and 46

1.14 Through this operation of sexuality and gender society takes up sets of meanings and organises them as masculinity or femininity, and lines them up with male or female bodies.

POLS/Fem 3 pp. 26–7

Appendix 2: Relationships

2.1 Different theoretical frameworks or understandings will place their focus on different relationships between power, agency and structure. For example, Structuralists and Post-Structuralists, such as Foucault, believe that most, if not all political outcomes are the result of structure or contextual factors. On the other hand, Intentionalists, such as Charles Taylor, see that actors have the ability to realise their own intentions and aspirations despite structural constraints.

2.2 If the collection of knowledge, data and statistics can determine a power relationship, then the withholding of that knowledge must also have a part to play in unequal power structures and relationships. My argument is that, for example, the very existence of detention centres and the manner in which they are run and presented to the public, limits the amount of knowledge Australian citizens have about detainees. This therefore limits the power that Australian citizens can have in relation to those in detention. Foucault explains this as 'modifying the field of information' which in turn can 'produce effects of power' [both these last quotes are from Foucault, 'The subject and power', in H.L. Dreyfus and P. Rabinow (eds), *Michel Foucault: Beyond Structuralism and Hermeneutics*, Chicago: University of Chicago Press, 1983, p. 218].

POLS/IR 15 pp. 8 and 12

2.3 The argument of this thesis is developed by demonstrating the following points:

i   *The power of discourse* —the way it can determine (alter, constrain, enable) the way an issue is conceived

ii The ability of issues to be *placed* within a particular framework/discourse

iii The effects of placing an issue within the particular discourse of security

iv The reasons why *asylum seekers* are particularly vulnerable to being represented as a security threat

v   How this process took place in the *Australian context* from 1999 to 2001

My argument is developed through an analysis of the language used by the government to construct an image of asylum seekers as 'the enemy'.

2.4 A discourse appears when language is structured around a set of terms which draw on a particular field of enquiry or discipline. This structure places boundaries on how an issue is approached so that a particular point of view comes to be seen as the 'common sense' point of view. Jennifer Milliken states 'discourses make intelligible some ways of being in, and acting towards, the world, and of operationalising a particular "regime of truth" while excluding other possible modes of identity and action'. In this thesis I will use the example of the placement of asylum seekers within a discourse of security to demonstrate how discourse defines, and often restricts, understandings of and responses to issues. A discourse is created when an issue is discussed using particular language and terms which position the issue within that discourse. [Reference is to Jennifer Milliken, 'The study of discourse in International relations', in *European Journal of International Relations*, 1993, p. 236.]

Quote from Hugh Mehan:

'Language has power. The language we use in public political discourse and the way we talk about events and people in everyday life makes a difference in the way we think and the way we act about them . . . words have constitutive power; they make meaning of things. And when we make meaning, the world is changed as consequence.' [Hugh Mehan, 'The discourse of the illegal immigration debate: A case study in the politics of representation', *Discourse and Society*, 1997, p. 250.]

2.5 Language is not just a descriptor; it is not simply a tool used in hindsight to describe action. Language is dynamic; it has an active quality. It acts upon the world. 'The constitutive view treats language as an active political force composed of "practices which systematically form the objects of which they speak"' [Mehan, 1997, p. 251]. It adopts the conventional principle which says meaning develops through the strategic application of discursive practices and strategies.

2.6 In effect, discourse produces the world; it renders logical and proper certain policies by authorities and in the implementation of these policies shapes and changes people's modes and conditions of living. Discourse determines what comes to be accepted as the 'common sense' way of thinking about an issue. In this way, discourse inevitably leads to certain courses of action; through language an elite's 'regime of truth' [makes] possible certain courses of action by a state . . . while excluding others policies as unintelligible or unworkable or improper. In this sense, as language produces the world, those in power—those who exert control over and shape the language in the public arena—influence the world and its thinking. Thus those who establish the discourse can exert an enormous influence on the way that issue is seen and can use discourse to legitimise a particular response.

2.7 . . . the establishment of the discourse of security in relation to asylum seekers helped justify and rationalise the sense of moral indignation that many felt towards asylum seekers. In this way the discourse of security legitimised the emotional response felt by many towards asylum seekers.

2.8 The ability of the national interest rhetoric to create a kind of imposed nationalism also facilitated the acceptance of the discourse of security. It made the Australian public receptive to the Australian government's representation of asylum seekers as a threat and led to the widespread public endorsement of the government's response to the issue.

2.9 'Law and order policy debates in NSW state politics in this period were underpinned by the linking of crime and ethnicity. Rhetoric that drew on fear—of otherness, of difference, of change—was reflected in media commentary, government policy and public debate.' [From Richard Phillips and Ruby Rankin, 'Australia: State Labor government and media attack on the Anti-Discrimination Board', on a *World Socialist Web* website.]

2.10 The Australian public's acceptance of the government's representation of asylum seekers as the 'threatening other' tapped into aspects of Australia's cultural history. It stirred . . . an underlying racist paranoia in Australian society. As McMaster states: 'The Australian public has become conditioned to fear the arrival of asylum-seekers, especially boat people, and this . . . both reinvigorates Australia's strain of racism and feeds into the underlying sense of insecurity in the populace'.

2.11 This 'narrative of paranoia' was actively reawakened by the government in relation to asylum seekers.

2.12 In summary this section has demonstrated that a discourse of security was established, by the Australian government, in relation to asylum seekers. It shows that the government established this discourse through its choice of language and symbols and primarily through positioning asylum seekers as a threat to Australia's borders and sovereignty. This example explored [*sic*] in this chapter clarifies the point made in chapter two: that language plays an active and key role in constructing an issue in a particular way and thus has a huge impact on the way in which the issue is approached.

POLS/IR 17 pp. 2, 6, 7, 8, 42, 46, 51, 59, 61, 74–5

2.13 The relationship between power and language is frequently overlooked, which impacts on the interpretation of knowledge (and truth) claims. This is because, as Foucault outlines in his discussion of power in *The History of Sexuality (Vol One)*, people fail to grasp the complexity of the power relations operating within their societies.

2.14 Thus whilst it is often acknowledged individuals do not have limitless choice, Foucault's poststructuralist conception of subjectivity draws attention to the limits imposed by language/discourse. Consequently, whilst individuals have agency, that is the capacity to choose one course of action over another, the power/knowledge nexus modifies these choices. Therefore, whilst individuals author their own speech

> 'One cannot speak of anything at anytime; it is not easy to say something new, it is not enough to open our eyes, to pay attention, or to be aware, for new objects suddenly to light up and emerge out of the ground.'
> [Quote from Foucault, *Archeology of Knowledge*, p. 49.]

Individuals are always situated within a particular context that frames their position in, and perspectives of, society. Foucault thus advocates a qualified form of agency without full autonomy.

2.15 Power determines what is possible to speak, so Howard too is constrained to an extent by discourses Australia's political culture has made available.

2.16 Language does not simply refer to reality; it *constructs* reality. **This is the student's general conclusion from the observation that:**

. . . prioritising the denotative meaning (which is fixed in reality) as legitimate over the connotative meaning (which is determined within discursive events) is only sustainable if language's function can be reduced to a referential tool for reality—a position I explicitly discredit in Chapter 1.

2.17 Significantly, highlighting how discourse shapes agents' discussion of political issues, is not to say we are trapped in language, unconsciously adopting pre-determined subject positions. It is rather simply to propose the focus of reform should not be in establishing public discourse's liberation from power, as if 'a state of communication that would allow games of truth to circulate freely, without any constrains or coercive effects' was possible. Instead, it advocates a focus on identifying the 'mobile and transitory points of resistance' present everywhere in the power network, which renders dominant discourses (and their subsequent knowledge claims) fragile . . . Thus instead of simply focusing on how Howard (and his government) control public debate—and subsequent representations of political issues—it becomes possible to acknowledge the extent to which language *prescribes the terms of the debate*. [Emphasis in original]

2.18 As an analysis of the House of Representatives parliamentary debate and media interviews demonstrates, the overwhelming majority of politicians . . . invoke the security debate in their discussion of asylum seekers. Within this discourse asylum seekers are constructed as 'unauthorised arrivals' rather than fellow human beings. This is because this discourse *produces* only a 'limited number of statements' about asylum seekers which preface [I think s/he means 'privilege'] the mode of arrival over the human agents involved in seeking political asylum. In this way then, this discourse limits the interpretation of boats in Australian territorial waters to only a breach of border security by foreclosing discussion of asylum seekers as a humanitarian problem. Thus by constructing asylum seekers as boats rather than human beings, the security of borders over the security of people is *regarded* (that is, accepted as) a legitimate rationalisation within this discourse.

2.19 Thus despite some contention over the purpose of the Migration Bill (2006), it is clear *both parties construct* asylum seekers as a problem that ought to be controlled by the Australian government. Thus *the production (and organisation of) knowledge claims about asylum seekers within this discourse, construct asylum seekers* as a foreign affairs problem requiring diplomacy rather than a human problem requiring compassionate solutions. [Emphases added]

The student author has not seen the potential contradiction between these two italicised formulations.

2.20 Despite the evident variation in the interpretation of asylum claims within the humanitarian discourse it is possible to identify two dominant assumptions that fix the limits of this discourse. First, within the discourse, all speakers assume Australia's capacity to provide humanitarian assistance *is* limited. The debate therefore focuses . . . on the establishment of who is most worthy of Australia's protection. Second the debate assumes the *Refugee Convention* provides sufficient protection for asylum seekers. In this way, then, the debate orientates itself around establishing whose claims correlate best with the requirements as outlined by the Convention without any discussion of how appropriate the treaty's criterion is. Again, I am not trying to argue resources are not limited or that the refugee definition is necessarily problematic. *I am rather highlighting that these assumptions restrict the scope of public debate within this discourse.* [Emphasis added]

This last formulation is correct. But who or what *makes* 'the assumptions'?

POLS/IR 18 pp. 28, 41, 54, 61, 62, 70–1, 75, 81

2.21 I want to examine how women can be positioned as subjects within the text and the audience. This text/spectator relationship then shapes how individual women construct their subjectivity.

I argue that the process of communication between text and spectator is not singular or one way. Rather popular culture offers a variety of representations and subject positions within texts that are negotiated and used by spectators in the construction of their subjectivities.

2.22 It is through discourses that subjects gain the knowledge and language to speak of and organise themselves and the social world . . . As subjects we are ultimately implicated by power and discourses and so cannot be exterior to them. Hence we can only speak as and be 'ourselves' within the definitions of self and identity produced and provided within discourses.

2.23 Discourses are, therefore, central in the discussion of subjectivity as they are the primary mechanism through which individual subjectivities are created, made intelligible and con-tested. As subjects are produced through discourses, there is no longer a sense of subjects as independent of discourses.

2.24 Power driven discourses produce and reinforce the meanings that create and that are embedded in subjectivity.

POLS/Fem 3 pp. 18, 19, 20 and 22.

Appendix 3: Power

3.1 Power and knowledge are mutually constitutive. Truth is a function of power. Ruling groups are able to assert a particular view of knowledge which is used to distinguish right from wrong. By way of example: medieval monarchical power provided an essential focus around which legal thought developed. In the service of royal power the judicial edifice of western states developed as a justification and instrument of that power. In this way the truth which is produced by power provides an understanding of the limits and rights of power. Therefore sovereignty can be understood as not a fixed notion of governmental authority. It is a constant right of power that evolves and develops to create new truth/knowledge to justify its changing character.

POLS/IR 4 p. 20

3.2 . . . Michel Foucault takes a different approach to the definition of power and examines how power is organised through its mechanisms. Power in this case is not from one actor to another, A to B, but is more diverse in nature. He describes the exercise of power 'through a net-like organisation in which individuals undergo and exercise power simultaneously'. [Reference to Foucault, 'Power', in Steven Lukes (ed.), *Power*, Blackwell, 1986, p. 234.] Power is exercised over human bodies and their operations as opposed to power exercised over goods and wealth. These 'disciplines' and 'discourses of truth' are the bearers of the effects of truth, and power produces the truths we acknowledge. 'In a society such as ours, but basically in any society, there are manifold relations of power which permeate, characterise and constitute the social body, and these relations of power cannot themselves be established, consolidated nor implemented without the production, accumulation, circulation and functioning of a discourse.' [Same reference.]

POLS/IR 5 pp. 13–14

3.3 Said's work draws heavily on the theories of Michel Foucault. Particularly important to Said's explanation of Orientalism is Foucault's idea that there is an intimate connection between power and knowledge. Foucault argued that knowledge can never be pure but rather is necessarily affected by the 'net like organisation' of power. He believed that discourses are part of this organisation through which power is employed and exercised,

> 'Power does not only weigh upon us as a force that says no but traverses and produces things, it induces pleasure, forms knowledge, produces discourses' [Quote footnoted as from Foucault, *Power/Knowledge*, C. Gorgon (ed.), NY: Pantheon, 1980, p. 131].

POLS/IR 11 p. 8

3.4 Understanding the productive element of power enables an analysis of the way that African societies were produced and then reproduced in representation. Also, power taken from this perspective generates an awareness of the divisive interests that constituted colonialism in Africa. Analysis of power and the inherent forms of resistance that embody power proceeds as a means of conceptualising the agency of the African people to shape colonialism, that is, to employ it for their own gain and to exercise choices within the structures of colonial power.

POLS/IR 12 pp. 15–16

3.5 . . . the academic literature's explanation of Howard's domination of the public debate is premised on the assumption that power can be (and is) fixed and localised in agents, in this case, Howard and his government. It fails to acknowledge therefore . . . that 'power is not acquired, seized or shared' but rather 'exercised from innumerable points in the interplay of nonegalitarian and mobile relations' [quotes are from Foucault's *History of Sexuality*, p. 94].

3.6 Power determines what is possible to speak, so Howard too is constrained to an extent by discourses Australia's political culture has made available.

3.7 Significantly, highlighting how discourse shapes agents' discussion of political issues, is not to say we are trapped in language, unconsciously adopting pre-determined subject positions. It is rather simply to propose the focus of reform should not be in establishing public discourse's liberation from power, as if 'a state of communication that would allow games of truth to circulate freely, without any constrains or coercive effects' was possible. Instead, it advocates a focus on identifying the 'mobile and transitory points of resistance' present everywhere in the power network, which renders dominant discourses (and their subsequent knowledge claims) fragile . . . Thus instead of simply focusing on how Howard (and his government) control public debate—and subsequent representations of political issues—it becomes possible to acknowledge the extent to which language *prescribes the terms of the debate*. [Emphasis in original]

POLS/IR 18 pp. 44 and 62

3.8 He [Foucault] proposes that power should not be considered a fixed property, and it is not an enduring characteristic of an individual subject within society. Rather, 'power is everywhere', not as a possession but as a relation. It is a dynamic situation that is immanent and continually exercised within the complex relations of individuals and society. It is positive and productive in its possibilities of choice and action, thereby producing the conditions for resistance and the exercise of autonomy. In fact freedom, according to Foucault, is not a realm outside of or unconstrained by power. There is no freedom from power for Foucault. Freedom is simply an effect of the exercise of power within the dynamics of discourse. In short freedom is a ruse of power.

3.9 Foucault focuses on the mechanisms that allow subjects to endorse and regulate the 'truth' of 'power' and 'knowledge'. Power exists in 'manifold relations(s) . . . which permeate, characterise, and constitute the social body . . . [which] cannot themselves be established, consolidated nor implemented without the production, accumulation, circulation and functioning of a discourse.'

> 'We must cease once and for all to describe the effects in negative terms: it "excludes", it "represses", it "censors", it "abstracts", it "masks", it "conceals". In fact power produces; it produces reality; it produces domains of truth. The individual and the knowledge that may be gained of him belong to this production.' [Quote from *The History of Sexuality*, vol. 1, London, 1990.]

3.10 Subjects themselves exercise power and are characterised by it. They are constituted through power such that the exercise of power does not require external surveillance or coercion. While he claims that subjects are normalised, 'responsibilised' and disciplined through the dynamics of power relations, he also asserts that individuals are subjective, autonomous agents. Foucault seems to be implying that individuals are animated by yet autonomous within discursive power. Through voluntary self-regulation and self-discipline they achieve and secure a subjective identity. So, we are subjected to power, but also autonomous within it? Foucault introduces this contradiction to allow for his all important possibility of resistance. However, it is a contradiction that Foucault neglects to resolve adequately, and one that causes feminists to question the lack of a normative framework for resistance.

3.11 His later understanding of power in *Power/Knowledge, The History of Sexuality Volume 1* and 'The Subject and Power' puts forward 'an agonistic model of power'—'a set of actions upon other actions' in which 'discourse transmits and produces power; it reinforces it, but also undermines and exposes it, renders it fragile and makes it possible to thwart it'. Resistance to power is the assertion of 'truth' that is also constituted by discourses, whether 'reverse discourses' or 'counter discourses' to the dominant discourse. He claims that in order for a relationship of power to exist, a subject must be capable of action or resistance and be recognised as a person on whom power is exercised.

3.12 . . . Foucault asserts that 'individuals continuously contest fixed identities and relations in subtle ways [quote from Foucault, *Power/Knowledge: Selected Interviews and other Writings 1972–77*]. That is, power through domination produces greater possibilities for resistance by subjects. However, if the possibilities for resisting power are contained within power itself, then where are the sites for resisting it located?

POLS/Fem 2, p. 16

3.13 [Foucault's] analysis of discourse opens up an understanding of the nature and location of power within different discursive regimes. This has allowed postmodern feminists to locate and establish alternate knowledge bases for the legitimacy of women, in view of different ethnic, class and sexual backgrounds.

3.14 Fraser argues that the crucial defect in Foucault's conception of power is that he does not provide a clear normative framework with which to apply his analysis. Furthermore his assertion that power is a capillary network, and that domination and subordination are effects of multiple power relations rather than the cause of a specific source of power, implies that all forms of power are normatively equivalent. This has raised much contention in feminism as it negates the legitimacy for women's experience of oppression under patriarchal domination, and thereby it is difficult to apply to the politics of women's daily life.

3.15 Foucault says that identity is produced through variable forces and discursive fields. Butler takes this one step further by claiming that, given that identity is an affect of power relations, it cannot be taken uncritically as the foundation on which, for example, feminists theorises [*sic*] and propose strategies for political ends for 'women'. . . . Coalitional politics which emphasises unity, like the theories of Bordo and Grosz, privilege unity over the fragmentation and conflict that may need to be recognised and left unresolved for a truer appreciation for the multiple identities of 'women' if that label can still be used.

POLS/Fem 2 pp. 7, 9, 14–15, 15, 19, 21, 22

3.16 Rather than being essentialist, Butler's politics are an elaboration of Foucault's work in *The History of Sexuality*, relying on his thesis that 'power produces(s) the subjects (it) subsequently come(s) to represent'. Her post-structuralist understanding of the subject, is that there is no 'political shape to "women" . . . that precedes and prefigure the political elaboration of their interests' thereby denying the existence of a pre-discursive subject that feminism could represent. For Butler, the subject is not rational or unified and has no essential identity; there is no knowing subject that exists outside of language/discourse. [Quotes are both from *Gender Trouble*, pp. 3 and 164].

POLS/Fem 4 p. 13

Appendix 4: The social construction of reality

4.1 Textuality is a powerful way to create the imagined community that is the nation and historical narratives are one of the most powerful textual forms of incorporation. History is commonly perceived as 'fact', and can be ascertained by thoroughly researching names and dates and places. However history lends itself to differing and often conflicting interpretations. Historical narratives can be constructed by interest groups to support political positions or objectives, and are often based on highly selective interpretations of historical evidence. As history is popularly perceived as fact, the shaping of history for political ends legitimises these positions or objectives. This is why the claim to represent the 'true' account of history is so contested by nationalists.

4.2 This chapter explores the ways in which the historical themes outlined in chapter two have provided the raw material for political discourse. It examines the discourses of those involved in the Aceh issue, shows which elements are privileged over others, why this is so, and how the discourses are structured to create concrete meanings.

The crucial phrase here of course is 'provided the raw material for', because what it suggests is that 'the raw material' is somehow epistemologically or ontologically *prior* to the said 'political discourse'.

And in fact everything that follows confirms this—what we are shown is that certain *facts* about (for example) Acehnese anticolonial heroism and struggle are not contested by *either* nationalists or integrationists or autonomists. What is contested is broadly *some* descriptors of those facts and *explanations* of them.

4.3 In contrast, integrationist discourse structures the same historical material in different ways to make Aceh's freedom loving character a referent for *Indonesian* nationalism.

But how does s/he know it is 'the same' historical material?

Page 49 demonstrates the same point:

4.4 The second important theme that emerges . . . is Aceh's Islamic identity. The earliest recorded conversions were in Aceh, and today Aceh is a staunchly Islamic region. *This theme is evident in the discourses of all three groups involved in the 'Aceh problem', although these discourses treat it in contradictory ways.* [Emphasis added]

How does s/he know that the 'it' is an 'it'? That is, what is 'it' that is 'treated' differently in the 'discourses' of the three groups? Presumably something that can be described or specified separately from these discourses. But from the student's theoretical point of view, this is a profoundly problematic answer.

POLS/IR 3 pp. 35 and 49

4.5 Power and knowledge are mutually constitutive. Truth is a function of power. Ruling groups are able to assert a particular view of knowledge which is used to distinguish right from wrong. By way of example: medieval monarchical power provided an essential focus around which legal thought developed. In the service of royal power the judicial edifice of western states developed as a justification and instrument of that power. In this way the truth which is produced by power provides an understanding of the limits and rights of power. Therefore sovereignty can be understood as not a fixed notion of governmental authority. It is a constant right of power that evolves and develops to create new truth/knowledge to justify its changing character.

POLS/IR 4 p. 20

4.6 Poststructuralism is text centred, and this is sometimes given such a broad meaning that it is often suggested that all the world can be read as a text. Texts, they suggest, have a plurality of meanings, thus no two texts are ever alike and no two readings of the same text are ever identical. At the same time, all texts are interrelated, thus poststructuralists talk of 'intertextuality'. Poststructuralists do not attempt to uncover an independent objective reality. That is, they do not seek to invoke rationality as a justification or explanation of certain interpretations. Neither is it hermeneutic, in the sense that there is a deeper, truer, meaning waiting to be discovered, all textual meaning is never finally decided. Consequently it is meaningless to seek one best interpretation, or to establish the authority of one interpretation over another. There are no facts, no proper meaning to words, no authentic vision of a text, in short no simple truths.

Pages 34–47, which are the opening of Part II of the student's thesis, are devoted to an outline of poststructuralist thought, and in particular to the ideas of Deleuze and Guattari. They are fascinating for propounding one 'deeply' wrong set of half truths after another. For example:

4.7 Powerful western nations use theoretical tools to describe the world of state relations, and because of the position they occupy in that assemblage of power, that then becomes the way the world is . . . they suggest that . . . there is no warranted and fixed relation between language and what it stands for, language is grounded in the potentiality of subversion, the outflanking of the exercise of language/power itself.

4.8 [Guattari and Deleuze's thought] . . . confronts the subject-object distinction of modern epistemology where a neutral and objective world is mirrored in the receptive mind of a passive subject. Rejecting this view, they argue that the perception of the world is mediated through discourse and a socially constructed subjectivity.

The entire chapter from which these quotations come is a perfect demonstration that really bright students are attracted to this stuff for some of the best reasons (opposition to naïve subject-object duality, insight into the limits of a picture of language as simply representational, grasp of the epistemological importance of the relation of language to praxis, etc.) but the intensity of their attraction makes them *careless*—with regard to both their characterisation of what they are opposing (especially the canard of 'positivism'), and to epistemological questions generally. They are especially careless with issues concerning the heterogeneity of the phenomena that are dealt with in truth and reality statements. They simply do not see that that heterogeneity severely affects the range of applicability of all 'constructivist' formulations. It also means that very many of our descriptive and explanatory uses of language contain both 'constructive' and more 'reflective' terms, often in bewilderingly complex combinations. Hence broad-brush assertions about the 'construction of social reality' always beg a mass of detailed questions. Take a simple sentence such as, 'He walked gloomily, distractedly, up the street, tripped over a half-brick and fell into a despondent heap on the pavement.' How much of the 'reality' invoked in that sentence is 'socially constructed'?

POLS/IR 10 pp. 16–17, 34–47

4.9 In undertaking a constructivist analysis of the refugee policies of liberal democratic states and their relationship with international refugee law, I rejected a positivist epistemological approach to empirical observation, which seeks to uncover fixed objective facts and clearly identifiable causes. Instead I adopted a more interpretive approach to empirical observation, which recognises the inherent subjectivity of *all* [my emphasis] knowledge and seeks to make sense of the transitory social world in which events took place.

Can s/he really mean 'all'?

POLS/IR 14 p. 2

4.10 Through an analysis of the strength and role of discourse, particularly the discourse of insecurity, I will endeavour to uncover the power of 'truth'. In essence, discourse can be understood as a coherent set of assumptions, beliefs and institutional practices which relates to a particular aspect of political or social life. I will use the term 'discourse' consciously as an alternative to 'ideology', as the former places a greater emphasis on practices, not just ideas. This proves particularly useful when analysing government polices and policy documents, as these often merge with political practice. As such, I will deconstruct the Howard government's engagement with the discourse of insecurity through an examination of recent legislation, policy initiatives and the rhetoric of its Cabinet Ministers [*sic*] in relation to asylum seekers.

Note how quickly here a promised analysis of 'practices' reduces in fact to an analysis of *words*—i.e., policy documents!

POLS/IR 16 p. 5

4.11 *A propos* **of 'the national interest'**

. . . the security discourse created a kind of *imposed nationalism,* in which failure to support the government's stance on asylum seekers could be positioned as un-Australian and unpatriotic. As Matt McDonald states 'evoking the narrative of security would contribute to a solidification of the Australian self, and unite the people of Australia behind its political leaders, who were working to protect Australians from this "threat" '. [Quote from Matt McDonald, 'Fear, security and the politics of representing asylum aeekers', *M/C: A Journal of Media and Culture*, vol. 5, no. 2, 2002, p. 1.] This is again evidence of the power of the security discourse as a tool for political actors.

4.12 'The ability of the national interest rhetoric to create a kind of imposed nationalism also facilitated the acceptance of the discourse of security. It made the Australian public receptive to the Australian government's representation of asylum seekers as a threat and led to the widespread public endorsement of the government's response to the issue.' [Quote from Mehan (see earlier ref. (2.4, 2.5)), p. 258.]

4.13 The illegal alien designation invokes a representation of people who are outside of society. The illegal alien designation invokes images of foreign, repulsive, threatening, even extra-terrestrial beings. The proposition was aimed, therefore, not at 'people like us', who are 'law abiding' and 'tax-paying citizens'. It was aimed at foreigners, people from outside our world, who are invading and threatening our lives, 'the quality of our life'.

Question. It was aimed, but did it hit or miss? Answer (by implication) 'It hit of course'. But how do we know that? *Because* the policies towards asylum seekers were pursued and popularly endorsed. But see how question-begging this answer is.

4.14 . . . the term 'illegals' removed any sense that these are people who are fleeing persecution, people who have suffered and therefore may be deserving of our compassion.

On this same page a Hugh Mackay attitude survey is adduced as evidence that the use of the term 'illegals' worked. These data apparently showed there was a 'widespread view that people who have arrived illegally . . . are likely to behave illegally once here'. Again, I'm sure there was such a view, but was it *simply* a product of the government's rhetoric?

4.15 Quote from Richard Jenkins:

'Politicians, the press, public officials, and interest groups, may combine in the development and promotion of "moral panics" about issues such as abortion, homelessness, street violence, illegal immigration, child abuse and so on. These

may be influential in the public constitution of a "problem",
in its identification with particular social categories—and
their identification with it—and eventually in the framing of policy responses.' [Quote from Richard Jenkins,
'Categorisation, identity, social process and epistemology',
Current Sociology, 2000, p. 19.]

**The first sentence is good I think (because it dilutes the top-down
'populace passively swallows government rhetoric' conception of
political language in favour of something a lot more genuinely
sociological and interactive). The last phrase is the usual cop out
through vagueness. But the student follows this up with another
quotation:**

4.16 'Law and order policy debates in NSW state politics in this
period were underpinned by the linking of crime and ethnicity.
Rhetoric that drew on fear—of otherness, of difference, of
change—was reflected in media commentary, government policy
and public debate.' [Quote from Richard Phillips and Ruby
Rankin, 'Australia: State Labor government and media attack
Anti-Discrimination Board' on a *World Socialist Web* website.]
**This quote hovers perfectly between implying that the link
between 'crime and ethnicity' was 'made' by the rhetoric, and the
view that it either 'reflected' or 'reinforced' pre-existing popular
views on this 'link'.**

POLS/IR 17 pp. 46, 48, 49, 51

4.17 Foucault argues knowledge (or meaning) is not determined by
reality, or fixed in convention, but is rather a constructed produce
of power relations. This is because, for Foucault, language does not
operate as an abstraction where a 'finite body of rules' (grammar)
authorises an 'infinite number of performances' (statements).
Rather language is transformed by power into discourses whereby
'specific rules of appearance' authorise 'a limited number of
statements' to the exclusion of others about a specific issue.

In this way then, discourses determine what can be said, and therefore known, about a particular issue in a particular context: it [*sic*] governs the status of statements, 'the way in which they are institutionalised, received, used, reused [and] combined together'.

4.18 Consequently, Foucault's examination of power's productive role in the formation of meaning refutes the assumption that meaning is conventional, arbitrary or fixed. As such, it is no longer possible to assume that language can be used for purely descriptive projects, as language and reality are mutually constitutive with a dynamic relationship determined by power. This understanding of language, though, should not be interpreted as a refutation of the existence of an objective (or otherwise) reality. I interpret the poststructuralist claim that all language is metaphorical as only an expression of the inherent problems with literal definitions and not an ontological claim. I am therefore not concerned with the existence or otherwise of reality itself, but rather how an interdependent relationship between language and reality impacts on the representation of political issues.

4.19 Language does not simply refer to reality; it *constructs* reality.

This is the student's general conclusion from the observation that:

. . . prioritising the denotative meaning (which is fixed in reality) as legitimate over the connotative meaning (which is determined within discursive events) is only sustainable if language's function can be reduced to a referential tool for reality—a position I explicitly discredit in Chapter 1.

POLS/IR 18 pp. 21–2, 23 and 54

These quotations compound a number of errors. Meaning is certainly not a synonym for knowledge, and even in the *Tractatus* (which the student is explicitly critiquing in all these quotations) Wittgenstein clearly distinguishes meaning from knowledge. In the *Tractatus* epistemology, human beings make 'knowledge claims' by advancing 'propositions' which assert 'how things are' and these propositions are made up of 'words' which get their meaning from the 'objects' in the world that they 'name'. The really problematic quotation however is the second, especially its closing sentence beginning, 'I am therefore not concerned . . .'. It is difficult to see how one can first 'not be concerned with the existence or otherwise of reality' and then postulate a relationship (whether 'interdependent' or of any other kind) between 'language and reality'. That is, the last part of the sentence implicitly reasserts what the first part has just bracketed!

Very interestingly, the notion of a relationship between an entity called 'language' and an entity called 'reality' (or 'the world') is at the centre of Wittgenstein's *Tractatus*. And in his later philosophy Wittgenstein came to think that it was precisely this way of setting up the issue that had led him most profoundly astray. That is, the *Tractatus* was supposed to have shown how language 'related' to the world, but Wittgenstein subsequently came to think this was nonsense. There is no need to 'relate' language to reality or the world, whether through 'power' or 'discourse' or anything else (the younger Wittgenstein favoured 'logic'). There is no need to do so because language is a part of reality, or the world, and it is human beings acting in the world, both with and through language, which makes this so. So in fact this student has *not* transcended *Tractatus* epistemology. S/he has simply reproduced it in a slightly altered form.

4.20 Discourses are systems of social knowledge. They are 'historically variable ways of specifying knowledge and truth' [quote from C. Ramazanoglu (ed.), *Up Against Foucault*, London: Routledge, 1993, p. 10]. They function as sets of rules and concepts which specify what does and does not count as knowledge, and what is and what is not true. The establishment of 'truth' maintains and reinforces the stability of an order of power.

Thus the order of knowledge, or discourse, is transformed into an order of social power. In other words, the theory of knowledge becomes the theory of power.

POLS/Fem 2, p. 10

This is a fascinating passage. It hovers almost perfectly poised between sociology of knowledge and epistemology. As the former it is unexceptional; as the latter it is completely question-begging.

4.21 An earthquake only has meaning, we only 'know' an earthquake because we also know things that are part earthquake (an earth tremor) or not earthquake (a relatively stable geological formation). There *is* no 'reality' accessible to us outside thought; an object has existence, but not one meaning which constitutes its reality. What gives an object reality is our thought, our 'knowing' of it. We endow 'reality' through 'naming' and we cannot name or know in this sense, outside of a discursive structure. The third point then, relates to the nature of the distinction between an earthquake and a social structure. This is precisely where the notion of materiality comes in: in the same way as we understand the earthquake, we can only understand the material ritual, for example, of a lecture, within the discourse of 'the modern university' referred to earlier.

(1) 'We endow reality through naming and we cannot name or know . . . outside of a discursive structure' is classical *Tractatus* epistemology. It is demolished by what Wittgenstein has to say in the *Investigations*.

(2) We do not 'understand the material ritual, for example, of a lecture' whether 'within discourse' or any other way. This is purblind cognitivism. Rather we sit *in* a lecture (or lecture theatre)—and look and listen and fidget and take notes, and find the airconditioning too cold—and we understand (or not) the lecture.

(3) It is true that we would not 'know' what a lecture was if we did not know what a university was (the 'meaning' of a

lecture in that sense) but that this is so has nothing to do with the 'material ritual' of a lecture. In fact the 'material ritual of a lecture' is a rather mysterious phrase. I take it to have something to do with the materiality of lecture theatres, or podiums, or lecturers or microphones, and with the actions that people perform with these material objects and within these material conditions. But it hardly makes any sense at all to say that we do, or have to, 'understand' such things cognitively. Rather, as already stated, we 'act' with and within these things and our acting shows our understanding of them. Cognitivists never have any conception of understanding that goes beyond what minds or brains are doing!

4.22 The student then quotes Mouzelis:

> 'Insofar as Laclau and Mouffe do not identify discourse with language . . . then I agree with their view that all institutional arrangements . . . are discursively constructed. *But there is absolutely no reason why one should link discursive construction with fragility and precariousness.*' [Emphasis added] [Quote from Nicos Mouzelis, 'Ideology and class politics, a critique of Ernesto Laclau', *NLR*, Nov–Dec 1978, p. 108.]

Nicos Mouzelis is usually a very sensible bloke, but even he is sloppy here. 'All institutional arrangements are discursively constructed' is, at the least, not self-evidently true, because its meaning is not unambiguous. It is true that what (for example) the Bank of England is, what happens there—how we would 'describe' all that—is a matter of discourse. But no amount of discourse will take you to the fifteenth floor of the Bank of England building if the lifts aren't working (even if we talk about lifts in language—give them a name, etc.). It is really just a question about being careful and precise about what one is saying, and often this kind of 'theory' is neither! It specialises far too much in the grandiloquent phrase or generalisation.

POLS/Misc 1 pp. 20, 21, 22–3

4.23 To the extent that linguistic selection appears 'natural', the 'real world' is created by language. Concepts are in this way objectified. The linguistic expression of an experience can make it appear as an empirical fact. If a concept or idea, through which certain features are selected, becomes habitualised, then experience becomes welded to the features of the concept, and takes on their characteristics . . .

It is the culture within which the language is spoken which enables certain conceptualisations to appear natural. Meanings, acquired in use, are 'only appropriate to and valid in the cultural context in which they occur' [Hawkes, *Metaphor*, p. 58]. The linguistic habits within a culture create what becomes the 'real world'.

The nature of language is therefore paradoxical. Language is a creation or institution of society, yet it is also central to the creation and maintenance of that society. It both represents and frames the values of a culture.

POLS/Misc 3 p. 7

This last quotation perfectly exemplifies what is in some ways the underlying problem/issue. Almost by definition the social sciences and humanities deal overwhelmingly with those areas of language that concern human actions, and the repetitive patterns of those actions (social and political 'institutions'). In these areas of language it is often true that 'reality' ('social', 'political', 'cultural', even 'economic' reality) is what it is said/ thought/written to be 'in language'. (That is, the uses of language involved form, accompany, analyse, facilitate, criticise, describe, etc., the human actions that make and remake the reality.) But there are other areas of language (often relating to physical reality) that are more 'reflective' or 'representational' than

'constructive' or 'constitutive'. In these areas we tend to say not that X is the case because it is 'said' to be the case, but that it is said to be the case because it 'is' the case. Not, it's a door because we say it's a door, but we say it's a door because it is a door. In a sense what we have here is Wittgenstein's classic 'one-sided diet of examples'. And, as always, such a 'one-sided diet' leads to philosophical (epistemological) errors and slips, even when (as in this case) it is part of excellent, judicious, political theory. The philosophical error derives from a mutually reinforcing syndrome—linguistic constructivism tends to lead to a focus on certain areas or regions of language use, and the (empirical) examples predominantly or overwhelmingly addressed in those regions then confirm or validate the said constructivism. It is not that this, *per se*, is wrong, but it really only works by ignoring or marginalising other types/regions.

This is not the only problem because even the distinction drawn above (between more 'constructive' and more 'representational' regions of language) is problematic. It is problematic because, as Wittgenstein emphasises, in virtually every description of reality there are physical and non-physical components or aspects. That is, a piece of wood is only a door because it is hung, open and closed—i.e., it is 'used' as a door. (It has a 'socially determined use' we might say, constructively, and this use is part of what makes it a door). Nonetheless, that it is a physical piece of wood is important. Wood, together with metal, plastic etc., can be physically formed into a door, whereas chewing gum or helium gas cannot be so formed, or (therefore) so used. And this physical/non-physical 'mixture' is also a feature of much social and political description, although this is less often noted, because it is not emphasised—in fact it is occluded—in the 'one-sided diet'. So a parliament can take a variety of physical forms, but (a) it cannot take an infinite variety of such forms (How could we use a parliament built at a subatomic scale?) and (b) it must take *some* physical form—otherwise people could not make certain uses of this 'political' institution. (They could not 'sit' in it for example, nor talk in it, nor send emails from it, nor claim travelling expenses for going to and from it.)

So are parliaments socially constructed? 'Yes and no' is the answer, and it is also the answer for states, media empires, UN organisations, political parties, theatre and drama productions, films, plays, dreams, novels, sexuality, legal systems, etc. (Perhaps it's true of everything, although what we might call 'the balance of yes and no-ness'—of construction *v* reflection—may be different from case to case or from groups of cases to groups of cases.)

Appendix 5: The social construction of subjectivity

5.1 Discourses are thus seen by Foucault as systems of meaning and representation which perpetuate the status quo, ensuring the dominance of certain existing power structures. Following this argument, Said therefore defines the discourse of Orientalism as a discourse of power, he believes that the knowledge that Europeans have about the Orient is not value free but rather predicated on institutions of power. He argues that the discourse of Orientalism grew out of Western colonial practices, the West has exercised power over the Orient not only directly through colonialism but also through the construction of both an official and popular discourse of othering [*sic*] and subordination.

5.2 'Such texts (the texts with the authority of Western academics and governments) can create not only knowledge but also the very reality they appear to describe. In time knowledge and reality produce a tradition or what Michel Foucault calls a discourse whose material presence or weight, not the originality of the author, is really responsible for the texts produced out of it.' [Cited as Said, *Orientalism*, p. 94. I think the bracketed phrase in the first line of the quote is the student's but this is not absolutely clear.]

5.3 In short, Said believes that the West's knowledge about colonised lands and the West's power over colonised lands are in fact connected. He therefore sees Orientalism as 'western style [*sic*] for dominating, restructuring and having authority over the Orient' [cited as *Orientalism*, p. 3]. Through discursive practices the Western world has been able to influence not only the way the Orient is perceived in the West, but also the way 'Orientals' see themselves. Partha Chatterjee also believes that western discourse is a way for the West to continues [*sic*] exercising power in its old domain.

5.4 'Europe and the Americas, . . . have thought out on our behalf not only the script of colonial enlightenment and exploitation, but also that of our anticolonial resistance and postcolonial misery. Even our imaginations must remain forever colonised' [!! *sic*]. [Cited as Ania Loomba, *Colonialism/Postcolonialism*, London: Routledge, 1998, p. 44.]

In the next paragraph, the student glosses as:

5.5 While the West can no longer exercise control over the Orient in the same direct manner it was able to in the imperial age, it can still exercise ideological power and maintain control over the representations and filtration of knowledge of 'Oriental' cultures. POLS/IR 11 pp. 8–9

5.6 . . . the status of Quebec as a 'distinct society' within Canada relies on a classificatory system which outlines what is to be included as part of Quebecois culture. The problem with this system of classification . . . is that it establishes a system of social control, whereby these same group characteristics are used to create norms of acceptable behaviour for its various members.

Of the Australian terms NESC (Non-English Speaking Country) and NESB (Non-English Speaking Background) used by the ABS, the student author says:

5.7 The use of this term, while attempting to better understand and identify individuals from other countries, cannot help but homogenise and essentialise the characteristics of each group which is then used to differentiate between the overseas born.

5.8 . . . the conventional post structural enterprise of deconstructing a coherent self has reduced the effectiveness of oppositional politics for the deconstructed subject.

5.9 Naficy argues that a celebration of the hybrid's ambivalent position toward essentialist identification disempowers the hybrid subject through its preference to remain within the liminal space of hybridity.

Question: What kind of 'celebration' is this and what kind of 'disempowerment'?

5.10 . . . the key lies in a re-interpretation of the poststructural reading of difference; a reinterpretation that can promote group interests while not essentialising group characteristics.

5.11 . . . Haber's acknowledgement of artificiality allows her recognition to accommodate change through redescription, in contrast, Taylor's recognition, in an attempt to preserve culture, has to essentialise group identity in order to demarcate what is to be preserved. This cultural objectification recognises ethnicity as a marker of distinctiveness which is then ossified to legitimate survival. As we have argued, this ossification of cultural identity has ultimately resulted in the death of ethnicity, whereby ethnic identity is ossified and appropriated to legitimise making demands on the state.

POLS/IR 13 pp. 22, 23, 41, 42, 46, 48–9

5.12 Thus whilst it is often acknowledged individuals do not have limitless choice, Foucault's poststructuralist conception of subjectivity draws attention to the limits imposed by language/discourse. Consequently, whilst individuals have agency, that is the capacity to choose one course of action over another, the power/knowledge nexus modifies these choices. Therefore, whilst individuals author their own speech:

'One cannot speak of anything at anytime; it is not easy to say something new, it is not enough to open our eyes, to pay attention, or to be aware, for new objects

suddenly to light up and emerge out of the ground.'
[Quote from Foucault, *Archeology of Knowledge*, p. 49.]

5.13 [p. 42 (contd)] Individuals are always situated within a particular context that frames their position in, and perspectives of, society. Foucault thus advocates a qualified form of agency without full autonomy.

The quotation from Foucault strongly suggests an underlying *Tractatus* or 'Augustinian picture' epistemology. To 'say something new' is, apparently, to name or identify 'new objects'. But as Wittgenstein says in the *Investigations*: "'We name things and then we can talk about them: can refer to them in talk."—As if what we did next were given with the mere act of naming. As if there were only one thing called "talking about a thing". Whereas in fact we do the most various things with our sentences . . .'. (*PI*, 27)

5.14 As an analysis of the House of Representatives parliamentary debate and media interviews demonstrates, the overwhelming majority of politicians . . . invoke the security debate in their discussion of asylum seekers. Within this discourse 'asylum seekers' are constructed as 'unauthorised arrivals' rather than fellow human beings. [For whom?] This is because this discourse *produces* only a 'limited number of statements' about asylum seekers which preface [I think s/he means 'privilege'] the mode of arrival over the human agents involved in seeking political asylum. In this way then, this discourse limits the interpretation of boats in Australian territorial waters to only a breach of border security by foreclosing discussion [for whom?] of asylum seekers as a humanitarian problem. Thus by constructing asylum seekers as boats rather than human beings, the security of borders over the security of people is *regarded* [by whom?] (that is, accepted as) a legitimate rationalisation within this discourse.

5.15 The dominant assumption informing the construction of asylum seekers as a diplomatic problem is that Australia ought to control who enters Australia. Thus whilst [the] *Migration Bill (2006)* and what it achieves, was contentious, all parties nevertheless assume Australia should 'beyond question' determine who enters Australia . . . whilst I am not trying to suggest that this concern is wrong or illegitimate, I am highlighting that such a concern is the result of a particular organisation of knowledge claims, which have become increasingly legitimate over the century, owing to the frequent invocation of such a claim by various Government officials. It is my contention therefore, that such a claim is (and continues to be) historically contingent *and not objectively true*.' [Emphasis added]

Again, the student is presenting him/herself as not accepting dominant assumptions, which, again, problematises their dominance. S/he does however, and rather unusually, recognise this in the thesis by later quoting Australian dissident MPs and journalists who also challenged or problematised these dominant assumptions. It turns out, however, that it was not the MPs or journalists (i.e, the people) who actually did this, but some 'things' called 'resistant voices':

5.16 For example, by constructing asylum seekers as desperate people fleeing horrific circumstances, these voices argue Australia is obligated to fulfil the 'ancient and universal virtue' of 'taking in a stranger in need'. In this way then, these voices interrogate the distinction between Australian and foreigners to suggest Australia ought to position its ethical responsibility to the 'weak and vulnerable', irrespective of nationality. This new construction therefore, renders fragile the otherwise self-evident stratification of protecting asylum seekers that informs the border security and immigration control issues and thus makes it susceptible to criticism and reformation. Significantly then, while this discourse is still contingent (that is, socially and culturally produced) and should not be interpreted as an unmediated reflection of reality, it nevertheless produces 'the effect of truth' which jars/challenges the self-evident status of knowledge claims produced in the dominant discourse.

POLS/IR 18 pp 41, 70–1, 77, 86

Clearly this last quotation raises the whole issue of philosophical relativism. (See Chapter 10 of the text for a discussion.) I just note here that what this student in particular seems especially concerned with are the sorts of political disputes which are not, or not necessarily, about what is or is not true, but in which multiple descriptions are given of reality, all of which are 'true' (in the sense of 'not in conflict with any known facts'), but which are conflictual in that they embody different political values or ethical priorities. These are indeed very philosophically interesting types of disputes, but they don't require one to bracket classical notions of truth or reality to deal with them. What they really require is an understanding that describing the world is itself an activity or practice, informed by varied purposes and priorities. (This is the position adopted by Wittgenstein in the *Investigations* and other later writings—see Chapter 7.) The student fails to see this, however, because s/he is, again very ironically, working with a classically *Tractatus* conception of description—i.e., description as a 'copying' or 'mirroring' or 'reflecting' of the world. Hence any statements about the world which are not 'descriptive' in this sense cannot be either true or false (the classical *Tractatus* position). But in fact descriptions are not simply 'reflections' of the world, and so there can be highly varied descriptions of the same reality, all of which are true.

5.17 . . . Butler believes that there is no polymorphous sexuality or androgyny, which exists prior to our sexed and gendered being. There is no 'essence' of 'woman' that can be argued for in the struggle against patriarchal system [*sic*] that has produced our gendered and sexed identity. There is no pre-discursive gender or sex. Nevertheless, Butler argues that what can, and does, occur is that the so-called 'essential' nature of sex and gender is challenged from within the mechanisms of the system, thereby destabilising it. She uses parody, one of the hallmarks of postmodern art, in the example of drag to illustrate this: 'In imitating gender, drag implicitly reveals the imitative structure of gender itself—as well as its contingency'. [Quote cited as from Butler's *Gender Trouble: Feminism and the Subversion of Identity*, London: Routledge, 1990, p. 137.]

POLS/Fem 2 p. 44

5.18 I want to examine how women can be positioned as subjects within the text and the audience. This text/spectator relationship then shapes how individual women construct their subjectivity. I argue that the process of communication between text and spectator is not singular or one way. Rather popular culture offers a variety of representations and subject positions within texts that are negotiated and used by spectators in the construction of their subjectivities.

5.19 It is through discourses that subjects gain the knowledge and language to speak of and organise themselves and the social world . . . As subjects we are ultimately implicated by power and discourses and so cannot be exterior to them. Hence we can only speak as and be 'ourselves' within the definitions of self and identity produced and provided within discourses.

5.20 Discourses are, therefore, central in the discussion of subjectivity as they are the primary mechanism through which individual subjectivities are created, made intelligible and contested. As subjects are produced through discourses, there is no longer a sense of subjects as independent of discourses.

5.21 Power driven discourses produce and reinforce the meanings that create and that are embedded in subjectivity.

5.22 As a society we are divided unequally along the lines of sex, sexuality and gender created through discourses. These systems of discourses not only conceptualise the human race into the binary opposites; male/female, masculine/feminine and heterosexual/homosexual, but they privilege the male over the female.

POLS/Fem 3 p. 26

The first sentence here is true and unexceptional, up to 'created through discourses'. But that clause itself and the following sentence are linguistically violently idealist and determinist. Taken literally they would mean that before human beings had language, or when they had only primitive forms of language, they were not divided into male and female. Apart from anything else, if this were true, it would make the author's own existence deeply problematic!

5.23 Quote from Butler:

> 'I do not deny certain biological kinds of biological difference. But I always ask under what conditions . . . do biological differences . . . become the salient characteristics of sex.' [From an interview with Judith Butler by Peter Osborne and Lynne Segal in *Radical Philosophy*, No. 67, 1994.]

The student author glosses this as:

5.24 Butler deconstructs notions of the body and the material, but this does not mean that she denies them. Her argument is that no body exists or can be known or understood outside of discourse, a certain 'cultural framing' always takes place. This is not to suggest that the body is only discourse, but that this is the way we encounter it given that language too is reliant on and enmeshed with the material. Kaufman-Osborn offers in analogy the bonsai tree. The bonsai clearly adopts its shape due to the meticulous hands of its gardener, who bends, shapes and prunes its direction. But its shape, its appearance, and also the ability of the gardener, are reliant on the tree's actual woodiness and leafiness, its actual matter. By analogy, the body's 'sex' is not an essential pre-discursive assumption, not simply a fiction that we can remove, language is shaped by the material and the material is shaped by language.

This is a very good example of the deployment of a kind of argumentative/rhetorical sophistication to make the ridiculous sound subtle. The main conceptual problem with it is its reduction of 'the biological' to 'the body'. If modern evolutionary biochemistry is even approximately right, 'the biological' involves molecules and atoms, bacteria and viruses, genes and genomes, brain cells, muscles and blood types as much as whole bodies. More importantly, it involves the behaviour of *masses* of organisms and animals (including the human animal) over *eons* of time. Some biologically driven human behaviour is clearly pre-linguistic in origin—i.e., it predates the human capacity for language use—so to that extent it is not, cannot be, 'discursively constructed', at least not if 'constructed' is understood in any causal or originating way. This is not to deny that once human beings became language-using creatures this did not have a profound effect on their conceptions of everything. It is just to say that, even after the development of language, human behaviour, human 'action', cannot be reduced to the conceptual or discursive. It is possible, for example, to conduct an erotic relationship with another human being on a purely 'conceptual' level—but try getting pregnant that way!

The following quotation offers another example of this kind of sloppiness, this time involving Althusser's concept of 'interpellation'.

5.25 For example, a police officer yells 'Hey, you there!' to a man in the street. The convention is that the police officer has authority and the man does not. Prior to the call, there is no social subject, and so the police officer is not merely reprimanding, but is part of the social formation of the subject.

Now everything here depends on what 'there is no social subject' means. The student's own use of the word 'man' in the preceding sentence implies that 'there is no social subject' does *not* mean 'there is no biologically male person present', so presumably what it means is 'there is no biologically male person subject to a social role of subordination to the policeman'. But as the very grammatical structure of that last sentence shows, this does not at all imply that there is no 'biologically male person present' before the yell. In other words, what is being claimed here is either self-evident and unremarkable (an assertion about how and when we play 'social roles'—an assertion of a type that has been standard in sociology for eons) or nonsense. And the same holds for a lot of pomoish 'theoretical' assertions. When they are true they are not new, and when they are genuinely new they are not true.

The student author has the same logical problem with:

5.26 By responding to the hail, the man recognises that the yell was directed at him, and in this recognition becomes a subject. Althusser argues that this is because the man has recognised that the hail was truly addressed to him, that it is he that was hailed and not someone else.

On the face of it this sentence is blatantly self-contradictory, i.e., the terms 'the man', 'he' and 'him' it contains cannot be used if what it asserts is true.

POLS/Fem 4 pp. 20, 21, 22.

Appendix 6: Language and discourse

6.1 Through an analysis of the strength and role of discourse, particularly the discourse of insecurity, I will endeavour to uncover the power of 'truth'. In essence, discourse can be understood as a coherent set of assumptions, beliefs and institutional practices which relates to a particular aspect of political or social life. I will use the term 'discourse' consciously as an alternative to 'ideology', as the former places a greater emphasis on practices, not just ideas. This proves particularly useful when analysing government polices and policy documents, as these often merge with political practice. As such, I will deconstruct the Howard government's engagement with the discourse of insecurity through an examination of recent legislation, policy initiatives and the rhetoric of its Cabinet Ministers [*sic*] in relation to asylum seekers.

POLS/IR 16 p. 5

Note how quickly here a promised analysis of practices, reduces in fact to an analysis of words!

6.2 The argument of this thesis is developed by demonstrating the following points:

i   *The power of discourse*—the way it can determine (alter, constrain, enable) the way an issue is conceived

ii   The ability of issues to be *placed* within a particular framework/discourse

iii The effects of placing an issue within the particular discourse of security

iv The reasons why *asylum seekers* are particularly vulnerable to being represented as a security threat

v How this process took place in the *Australian context* from 1999–2001

My argument is developed through an analysis of the language used by the government to construct an image of asylum seekers as 'the enemy'.

6.3 A discourse appears when language is structured around a set of terms which draw on a particular field of enquiry or discipline. This structure places boundaries on how an issue is approached so that a particular point of view comes to be seen as the 'common sense' point of view. Jennifer Milliken states 'discourses make intelligible some ways of being in, and acting towards, the world, and of operationalising a particular "regime of truth" while excluding other possible modes of identity and action'. In this thesis I will use the example of the placement of asylum seekers within a discourse of security to demonstrate how discourse defines, and often restricts, understandings of and responses to issues. A discourse is created when an issue is discussed using particular language and terms which position the issue within that discourse. [Reference is to Jennifer Milliken, 'The study of discourse in International relations', *European Journal of International Relations*, 1993, p. 236.]

POLS/IR 17 pp. 2 and 6

6.4 Laclau and Mouffe insist that every discursive structure must be understood as material, that is, its character is not simply linguistic. Articulatory practice 'cannot consist of purely linguistic phenomena; but must instead pierce the entirely material density of the multifarious institutions, rituals and practices through which a discursive formation is structured' [quote is from E. Laclau and C. Mouffe, *Hegemony and Socialist Strategy*, London: Verso, 1985, p. 109].

Norman Geras does not seem to have grasped this aspect of their position. He rejects as 'shamefaced idealism' their assertion that 'every object is constituted as an object of discourse' (HSS, p. 108). Illustrating his objection, Geras informs us that we must recognise that (for example) an earthquake's reality is not determined by discourse (i.e. that there is a '*pre*-discursive objectivity or reality') unless we also believe that 'earthquakes would cease to happen should humanity perish'. Laclau and Mouffe argue that he is confusing the 'mere existence' ('being') with the reality ('entity') of an object. And they are right; Geras is in fact collapsing 'reality' into 'existence'.

But this is followed *directly* by:

6.5 An earthquake only has meaning, we only 'know' an earthquake because we also know things that are part earthquake (an earth tremor) or not earthquake (a relatively stable geological formation). There *is* no 'reality' accessible to us outside thought; an object has existence, but not one meaning which constitutes its reality. What gives an object reality is our thought, our 'knowing' of it. We endow 'reality' through 'naming' and we cannot name or know in this sense, outside of a discursive structure. The third point then, relates to the nature of the distinction between an earthquake and a social structure. This is precisely where the notion of materiality comes in: in the same way as we understand the earthquake, we can only understand the material ritual, for example, of a lecture, within the discourse of 'the modern university' referred to earlier.

POLS/Misc 1 pp. 20–1

6.6 I argue that an overly narrow definition of the notion of 'discourse' lies behind the claim that dance lacks meaning. Such narrow definitions are based on a linguistic understanding of discourse, as that of a written or spoken word . . .

6.7 Broadly defined 'discourse' encompasses three things. Firstly, it entails the communication of beliefs (cognition); secondly, it is a form of social communication; and thirdly, it is the study of the way in which language is used, in which communication and interaction are related to the social context. [At 'word' and at 'context' there are references to Teun. A. van Dijk (ed.), *Discourse as Structure and Process*, London: Sage, 1997.]

6.8 Postmodern dance is also discursive in that communication occurs through its specific structural framing—the aesthetic and expressive elements of dance interrelate with, and inform, the content. As the conventional signs and codes of postmodern dance are reframed, there is a degree of latitude in determining the new, recontextualised meaning of a 'sign' or 'code'. A discursive analysis of postmodern dance also reveals that, in the wider context of performance, the audience partially contributes to the meaning. The combination of the close audience-performer relationship and the open-ended nature of the text of postmodern dance result [*sic*] in works with multiple layers of meaning.

This is all very good, and does indeed reflect the original 'beyond language' meaning of the discourse concept. But the real issue is still what, having set the concept up in this way, you are *going to say about and with it, in language*, which can 'do justice' to its non-linguistic components. The difference between first-person and third-person forms of speech is vital here, and an aspect often missed.

6.9 The history of western theatre dance up until the twentieth century has involved the objectification and distancing of dance from reality, and has thereby encouraged the perception that dance is unable to independently engage in any meaningful discourse about reality.

6.10 I argue that the phrase 'the meaning of dance' is not a misnomer that it is historically assumed to be, as understood in terms of the 'translatability dilemma' of dance. Although the meanings accrued to words are relatively stable; have been historically certified through time; and are more direct and unambiguous than the meanings of human movement, this does not mean that dance lacks meaning. All that it indicates is that the specific properties of the language of dance differ from the properties of language in its generic form.

6.11 The inapplicability of the representational model to western theatre dance indicates that language, *broadly defined as discourse* [! emphasis added], is not always structurally linear. Furthermore, to posit the idea of a representative force of language, in terms of the linearity between the sign and the signified, is to narrowly define language. It is also to presuppose that language is restricted to the written and spoken word. I argue that to try to conflate the meaning of dance with the meaning of language (narrowly defined) is to assume that they are structurally similar (in terms of their abstract functions).

In terms of the abstract functions of language, dance primarily engages the aesthetic and expressive abstract functions [of what? of language?]; whilst the spoken and written word primarily engages the informative, the propositional and the persuasive abstract functions of language. The content and meaning of dance emerge through the interaction of aesthetic and expressive elements. I argue that meaning in dance is often not directly conveyed, as compared to the communicative force of the informative, propositional and persuasive abstract functions of the written and spoken word, but this does not reduce the extent of its meaning.

POLS/Misc 2 pp. 5, 6, 10, 11

Notes

Preface

[1] Some people might see it as strange and surprising that I could have seen these commitments—to Marx and to a classical conception of truth—as consistent. There is no contradiction, however. Marx *did* adhere to the classical conception, despite his views on ideology. That is, he believed that ideas could be both true and ideological and thus that the ideological use of ideas was an entirely separate matter from their truth. Despite what is commonly believed, therefore, when Marx states that some idea or body of ideas is 'ideological' he is not, or not necessarily, claiming that it/they are false. On this see Leszek Kolakowski, 'Karl Marx and the classical definition of truth' in his *Marxism and Beyond*, London: Paladin, 1969, pp. 59–87.

Introduction

[1] For the ethical and procedural dilemmas that this fact poses for supervisors and some suggestions on how to deal with them, see Chapter 11 ('Tips for teachers and supervisors').

[2] It is frequently said that this is not true because once students leave the university they quickly forget most of the 'exotic' ideas they have been taught there, including, indeed especially, 'theoretical' ideas. It is often added that, in any case, these ideas are only mastered for the sake of 'jumping through the hoops' to obtain high marks or good degrees. However, my view is that if students simply spout these ideas, cynically

and instrumentally, while studying and then forget them immediately they leave the university, that is even *more* damaging than if they are actually convinced of the truth of the ideas, at least to the society of which they are a part, if not to the students themselves. It is more socially damaging because such cynical attitudes reinforce the patronising conception of the university as a 'remote', 'impractical' ivory tower, even among university alumni. Readers may readily infer why I think such a patronising conception is so socially and politically damaging from Chapter 10 of this book, on 'the Enlightenment project'.

[3]   In the Australian system a distinction mark equates to an upper second class honours level, and a higher distinction mark—85% or better—to a first class honours level.

[4]   I should emphasise that I do *not* think such grades were wrong or undeserved. On the contrary, the kind of sophisticated intellectual errors and confusions identified in the following pages could only have been made by excellent students. In a way such mistakes are in themselves evidence of that excellence. My view, following Wittgenstein, is that all the theses reviewed are 'deeply' or 'profoundly' wrong, i.e., wrong in an important or worthwhile way, not in a stupid or obvious or uninteresting way. (For Wittgenstein's regular tendency to employ the notion of 'deep' or 'profound' mistakes as a kind of back-handed compliment, see M. O'C. Drury, 'Some notes on conversations with Wittgenstein', in Rush Rhees (ed.), *Recollections of Wittgenstein*, Oxford: Oxford University Press, 1984, p. 80, and Ray Monk, *Wittgenstein: The Duty of Genius*, London: Jonathan Cape, 1990, pp. 310 and 478).

[5]   The work of Jurgen Habermas, with its very strong philosophical content, is a major exception to this generalisation, but I class Habermas with the analytical tradition in political theory here because his substantive political positions, being classically liberal, engage very easily with that tradition. Indeed Habermas is the one major 'continental' theorist that Anglo-Saxon political theorists take seriously.

[6]   Gavin Kitching, *Wittgenstein and Society: Essays in Conceptual Puzzlement*, Aldershot: Ashgate, 2003, p. 176.

[7]   'Former' because in 2007, as part of a faculty restructure, the school was merged with three others into a new School of Social Sciences and International Studies.

Chapter 1

[1] In English sentence structure, subjects tend to precede predicates in word order. This, however, is a contingent feature of English as a relatively uninflected language. In other languages predicates can precede subjects, but this does not alter the *logical* relation of subjects to predicates.

Chapter 4

[1] It was the founding protocol of what is generally termed 'the linguistic turn' in philosophy which occurred, almost simultaneously, in Britain and parts of Europe in the years before the First World War. See R. Rorty (ed.), *The Linguistic Turn: Essays in Philosophical Method*, Chicago: University of Chicago Press, 1967.

[2] Although this is to be somewhat generous. There seems to have been some overt lying by the Australian government in the case of the 'children overboard' events, a point which the author of POLS/IR 18 acknowledges at the beginning of his/her thesis but, significantly perhaps, does not return to.

[3] For the later Wittgenstein on 'seeing as', see *PI*, 74, 228 and pp. 193–208. *PI* is Ludwig Wittgenstein, *Philosophical Investigations*, Oxford: Basil Blackwell, 1953. The numbers cited refer to the numbered remarks which make up the text and not to pages—unless otherwise stated.

[4] Stanley Cavell is very good on these kinds of disputes and issues. See Stanley Cavell, *The Claim of Reason: Wittgenstein, Skepticism, Morality and Tragedy*, Oxford: Oxford University Press, 1979, especially Chapter 9, pp. 247–73.

Chapter 6

[1] On this, see my *Wittgenstein and Society: Essays in Conceptual Puzzlement*, Aldershot: Ashgate, 2003, pp. 50–7.

[2] Ludwig Wittgenstein, *Zettel* (2nd edn), Oxford: Basil Blackwell, 1981. Again the number refers to a remark, not a page.

[3] At least not so long as both representations were drawn accurately to scale.

[4] 'We remain unconscious of the prodigious diversity of all the everyday language-games because the clothing of our language makes everything alike': *PI*, p. 224.

Chapter 7

[1] G. Kitching, *Wittgenstein and Society: Essays in Conceptual Puzzlement,* Aldershot: Ashgate, 2003, especially essays III, IV and V. See also T.P. Uschanov, 'Ernest Gellner's criticisms of Wittgenstein and ordinary language philosophy', in G. Kitching and N. Pleasants (eds), *Marx and Wittgenstein: Knowledge, Morality and Politics*, London: Routledge, 2002, pp. 23–46.

[2] On this, see, for example, M.B. Ostrow, *Wittgenstein's* Tractatus: *A Dialectical Interpretation*, Cambridge: Cambridge University Press, 2002; Michael Kremer, 'On the purpose of Tractarian nonsense', *Noûs*, vol. 35, no. 1, 2001, pp. 39–73; and A. Crary and R. Read (eds), *The New Wittgenstein*, London: Routledge, 2000, especially the two pieces by Cora Diamond and the piece by James Conant. On the whole, however, I am unpersuaded by the so-called 'resolute reading' of the *Tractatus*, which tends to underlie this revisionist stress on the continuities between the *Tractatus* and the *Investigations*. See my essay, 'Resolutely ethical: Wittgenstein, the dogmatism of analysis and contemporary Wittgensteinian Scholarship', in *Wittgenstein and Society, op cit.*, pp. 179–215. I do, however, endorse other aspects of 'the new Wittgenstein', especially the emphasis on the strong ethical dimension in all of his philosophy—early and late—and, most importantly, the conception of the later Wittgenstein's philosophical *method* and its 'therapeutic' point or purpose. On this see the important review article, 'Whose Wittgenstein?' by Phil Hutchinson and Rupert Read in *Philosophy*, vol. 80, 2005, pp. 432–55.

[3] For some of Wittgenstein's own comments on this intellectualisation, see for example *PI*, 46–7 above, and also 134–6.

[4] And indeed Wittgenstein acknowledges that. 'For a *large* class of cases—though not for all—in which we employ the word "meaning" it can be explained thus: the meaning of a word is its use in language' (*PI*, 43, emphasis in the original). But he does not help us by saying *anything* about the (presumably) smaller class of cases where meaning is *not* to be identified with use.

[5] Personally I have always preferred the 'fibres in a rope' analogy to the much more commented-upon 'family resemblance' analogy, because it makes it clearer (at least to me) *how* 'extended' meanings can be

connected to an original meaning without overlapping with it. In the latter analogy, we are invited to think of members of a family who have facial resemblances in common. Thus B has a shape of nose in common with A; C has a type of lips in common with B (but a completely different nose from A or B); D has nose and lips and eye shape in common with A, B and C; E inherits A's nose, but no features from B, C or D; and F has the lip shape of B and C but no facial feature in common with A. Thus we can connect A and F by *tracing* a pattern of facial resemblances, but F and A have *no* facial features in common. See *PI*, 67, for both analogies—readers can decide which they prefer!

It must also be said that the noun form itself—'meaning'—may be problematic here. In one way 'X has the meaning Y' is just a synonym for 'X means Y'. But the first form of this proposition tempts us to ask questions such as, 'What *is* this meaning?'; 'How did it *get*, or how can it *have*, this meaning?'; 'Can this meaning *be changed*?'; 'How can we *make* the meaning *clearer*?' which tend to make 'meaning' seem more and more like the name of a *substantive*. More importantly, the noun form may tempt us to think that meaning is some*thing* (some abstract 'thing') about which we should or might have 'a theory'. Thus the later Wittgenstein has often been said to present a 'use theory of meaning'. But, for example, if I say, 'How amazing! I mean, I've never seen anything like that before', *nobody* will think that they will understand my amazement better, or know more about why or how it is that I have 'never seen anything like that before', by or through 'a theory of meaning'! Here the proposition 'To mean something is a kind of *action* and therefore more like an *event* or *episode* than a thing', can be clarifying or therapeutic. One might say of meaning, in fact, what Wittgenstein says of intention, namely that it is, grammatically, a subsistent thing or entity, but that in fact 'it does not have genuine duration': *Zettel, op. cit.*, 45. See also the very well-known early passage from *The Blue and Brown Books*: 'The questions "What is length?", "What is meaning?", "What is the number one?" etc. produce in us a mental cramp. We feel that we can't point to anything in reply to them and yet ought to point to something. (We are up against one of the great sources of philosophical bewilderment: a substantive makes us look for a thing that corresponds to it.)' in L. Wittgenstein, *The Blue and Brown Books: Preliminary Studies for the 'Philosophical Investigations'*, Oxford: Basil Blackwell, 1969, p. 1.

6   On the face of it this may appear to be rather less true of Derrida, with his famous, or infamous, conception of the endless *différance* of meaning. But in fact Derrida operates with a conception of language that is just as unitary, and just as narrowly 'linguistic' as anything found in Foucault or Deleuze. The only difference is that Derrida's conception of the unity of language is blanketly *indeterminate*, i.e. leads him to blanket, universalistic assertions about *indeterminacy* of meaning which are as unwarranted and, in their own way, as 'imprisoning' as any of Foucault's deterministic formulations about 'discourse'. The most fundamental problem is the same in *all* these cases in fact—a contemplative AP/Tractatus focus on language, and thus on text—rather than an action-related focus on language *use*. When we examine language use we see that it is as unwarranted to say that all meanings are indeterminate as to say that they are all determinate. On this, see 'Tangents: Marx, Wittgenstein and Postmodernism' in my *Wittgenstein and Society*, *op cit.*, pp. 117–50.

Chapter 8

1   For two sympathetic introductions, see Ted Benton, *The Rise and Fall of Structural Marxism: Althusser and His Influence*, London: Macmillan, 1984; and Gregory Elliott, *Althusser: The Detour of Theory*, London: Verso, 1987. For a rather less sympathetic treatment, see my *Marxism and Science: Analysis of an Obsession*, University Park, PA: Penn State Press, 1994, pp. 62–102.

2   For an account of why it was confused, and why Marx was *not* an economic reductionist—because nobody coherently can be—see my *Marxism and Science, op cit.*, pp. 62–72. See also my *Karl Marx and the Philosophy of Praxis*, London: Routledge, 1988, Chapters 6 and 7, and David Rubinstein, *Marx and Wittgenstein: Social Praxis and Social Explanation*, London: Routledge & Kegan Paul, 1981, Chapters 5–8.

3   Not surprisingly given that—as he has subsequently admitted—when he offered his critique of 'humanist' and 'reductionist' Marxism, he had read very little Marx! See Louis Althusser, *The Future Last Forever: A Memoir*, New York: New Press, 1993.

4   The principal texts involved are Louis Althusser and Etienne Balibar, *Reading Capital*, London: New Left Books, 1970; Louis Althusser, *For*

Marx, London: Verso, 1977; and Louis Althusser, *Lenin and Philosophy and Other Essays*, London: New Left Books, 1977.

⁵ 'A main cause of philosophical disease—a one-sided diet: one nourishes one's thinking with only one kind of example': *PI*, 593.

⁶ See John Searle, *Speech Acts*, Cambridge: Cambridge University Press, 1969, for the founding text in this tradition, although several of John Austin's philosophical essays preceded Searle substantively. See especially Austin's *How to Do Things with Words*, Oxford: Oxford University Press, 1965.

⁷ For a treatment of Wittgenstein's entire thought, which makes this analogy central, see R.J. Ackerman, *Wittgenstein's City*, Amherst: University of Massachusetts Press, 1988.

⁸ P.A.T. Gasking and A.C. Jackson, 'Wittgenstein as teacher' in K.T. Fann (ed.), *Ludwig Wittgenstein: The Man and His Philosophy*, New York: Dell, 1967, p. 51. See also, and just in passing, 'Language is a labyrinth of paths. You approach from one side and know your way about: you approach the same place from another side and you no longer know your way about': *PI*, 203.

⁹ G. Kitching, *Wittgenstein and Society: Essays in Conceptual Puzzlement*, Aldershot: Ashgate, 2003, pp. 77–8.

Chapter 9

¹ A third possibility is that the students simply do not know what they are doing when they make these kinds of universalist assertions or that they are totally confused about this. And this might be so in some cases. But again I think it would simply be patronising to assume that it is true in all cases.

² I still think that the best single text arguing this case is Hugh Stretton, *The Political Sciences*, London: Routledge & Kegan Paul, 1969.

Chapter 10

¹ The literature on the Enlightenment is vast, and increasingly contentious, especially in the wake of Foucault's assault upon it. The beginning student, wanting a range of views from the traditional to the oppositional, and various points between, might consult as a starting point, Peter Gay, *The Enlightenment, An Interpretation* (2 vols),

and especially volume 2, *The Science of Freedom*, London: Weidenfeld & Nicolson, 1970; Michel Foucault, 'What is Enlightenment?' in P. Rabinow (ed.), *The Foucault Reader*, New York: Pantheon Books, 1984, pp. 32–50; Robert Wokler, 'The Enlightenment project and its critics', in S.E. Liedman (ed.), 'The Postmodernist Critique of the Project of Enlightenment', *Poznam Studies in The Philosophy of the Sciences and the Humanities*, vol. lviii, 1998, pp. 13–30; and Karlis Racevkis, *Postmodernism and the Search for Enlightenment*, Charlottesville: University of Virginia Press, 1993. Isaac Kramnick (ed.), *The Portable Enlightenment Reader*, New York: Viking, 1995, contains most of the essential historical texts, while Roy Porter, *The Creation of the Modern World: The Untold Story of the British Enlightenment*, New York: Norton, 2000, is a balanced and magisterial survey of both the British eighteenth-century Enlightenment and the contemporary debates surrounding the Enlightenment. For the latter, see especially his 'Introduction' (pp. xvii–xxiv) and Chapter 1 (pp. 1–23).

[2] An oft-quoted example of this was the 'miasma' theory of infectious disease influential in the nineteenth century. This belief held that human beings became sick through inhaling the 'miasmic' vapours and stench given off by open drains and sewers. Belief in this theory was used to justify the construction of closed, underground sewer pipes. We now know that the miasma theory was technically incorrect (infection was due to exposure to bacteria not to inhalation itself) but, by good fortune, the theory led to the 'correct' remedy for radically reducing human exposure to bacterial infection.

[3] On this, see for example, Roy Porter, *The Making of the Modern World*, *op. cit.*, pp. 219–28.

[4] For a polemical argument about this, which is not the less true for being polemical, see Richard Dawkins, *The God Delusion*, London: Bantam, 2006, pp. 360–74.

[5] Anyone doubting this should read, for example, Joseph Needham's encyclopaedic account of Chinese science and technology: Joseph Needham, *Science and Civilisation in China*, Cambridge: Cambridge University Press, 1956–2004. For a modern, popular account, see also John Hobson, *The Eastern Origins of Western Civilisation*, Cambridge: Cambridge University Press, 2004.

[6] In other words it is right and proper to say that the pursuit of truth

is a virtue that must, in certain circumstances, be subordinated to other virtues—showing respect and regard for our fellow human beings, or for other animals, for example. That is to say, the pursuit of truth is not a virtue which should be prioritised in *all* circumstances and in disregard of *all* other virtues. Indeed, as I have argued elsewhere, *no* human virtue should be prioritised in *all* circumstances and irrespective of *all* other virtues: see G. Kitching, *Wittgenstein and Society: Essays in Conceptual Puzzlement*, Aldershot: Ashgate, 2003, pp. 102–5. And that is precisely why really important ethical or moral decisions can be so agonising. They are agonising, that is to say, in specific circumstances which make choosing *which* virtue or value should prevail exceptionally difficult. And when such choices are exceptionally difficult equally well-intentioned people can argue, equally reasonably, for different orders of moral priority. The important point, however, when deciding to give the pursuit of truth a lower value than some other good, is to say: 'I/we are giving the pursuit of truth a lower value than morally desirable situation X' and *not* 'if this truth conflicts with morally desirable situation X it is not true'.

7   By which I mean not only that it exposed them to the hostility and ridicule of others, but that pursuing the truth often involved them in painful psychological and emotional conflicts with *their own* religious beliefs and feelings. On this see, for example, Arthur Koestler, *The Sleepwalkers*, Harmondsworth: Penguin, 1964, Parts 4 and 5.

8   On this see, for example, Dawkins, *op. cit.*, pp. 113–51.

9   Kant chose a Latin tag from the poet Horace—*sapere aude*—'dare to know'—to indicate the importance of people thinking for themselves in his conception of enlightenment: I. Kant, 'What is Enlightenment?' (1784) in Isaac Kramnick (ed.), *op. cit.*, pp. 1–7. This seems very apposite. The great Enlightenment thinkers were very daring. They thought that human beings could take wing on reason. Having witnessed some very nasty crashes, however, many postmodern thinkers see such daring and courage simply as foolhardiness or hubris. This is why, rather than take wing from the cliff edge on the abseil of reason and science, they crouch nervously behind a relativist boulder.

10   Most notably in *The Archeology of Knowledge*, London: Tavistock, 1972, especially Part IV, Chapters 4, 5 and 6.

11   A. Sokal and J. Bricmont, *Intellectual Impostures: Postmodern*

Philosophers' Abuse of Science, London: Profile Books, 1998, pp. 183–5, fn. 258.

[12] Jurgen Habermas has insisted on this point—at great length—especially in his two-volume *Theory of Communicative Action*, Boston: Beacon Press, 1984. See particularly volume 1, pp. 8–42. For comments, see Anthony Giddens, 'Reason without revolution? Habermas's *Theorie die kommunikativen Handelns*' and Jurgen Habermas's 'Questions and counterquestions', in Richard J. Bernstein (ed.), *Habermas and Modernity*, Cambridge: Polity, 1985, pp. 95–121 and 192–216; and the very interesting discussion of communicative action in Nigel Pleasants, *Wittgenstein and the Idea of a Critical Social Theory: A Critique of Giddens, Habermas and Bhaskar*, London: Routledge, 1999, pp. 149–58.

[13] It also, of course, required *personal* courage to continue to pursue and advocate truths in the face of powerful opposition and even persecution.

[14] Wittgenstein himself thought that might be the case. In 1948 he wrote: 'It isn't absurd, e.g., to believe that the age of science and technology is the beginning of the end for humanity, that the idea of progress is a delusion, along with the idea that the truth will ultimately be known; that there is nothing good or desirable about scientific knowledge and that mankind in seeking it, is falling into a trap. It is by no means obvious that this is not how things are': Wittgenstein, *Culture and Value*, edited by G.H. von Wright in collaboration with Heikki Nyman, trans. Peter Winch, Oxford: Basil Blackwell, 1980, p. 56e.

Chapter 11

[1] Walter Bagehot, *The English Constitution*, London: Fontana/Collins, 1963 [1867], p. 111.

[2] Principally because they can be used as a word-saving *shorthand*. 'This perspective emphasises . . .' is a way of generalising about ideas shared by a large number of people which does not involve one in enumerating all the people or all the variations in the idea shared.

[3] 'And we do here what we do in a host of similar cases: because we cannot specify any one bodily action which we call pointing to the shape (as opposed, for example, to the colour), we say that a *spiritual* [mental, intellectual] activity corresponds to these words.

Where our language suggests a body and there is none: there, we should like to say, is a *spirit*': *PI*, 36, emphasis in the original. See also the very well-known early passage from *The Blue and Brown Books*, quoted in full in Chapter 7, which ends 'We are up against one of the great sources of philosophical bewilderment: a substantive makes us look for a thing that corresponds to it.'

4   This implies, as indeed I have already said, that this kind of theoretical discourse is profoundly 'reificatory', and there is much that could be said about this. Just for a start, readers are referred to Ferruccio Rossi-Landi's brilliant essay in which Wittgenstein is seen as an analyst of human alienation as this expresses itself in linguistic reification: F. Rossi-Landi, 'Toward a Marxian use of Wittgenstein', in G. Kitching and N. Pleasants (eds), *Marx and Wittgenstein: Knowledge, Morality and Politics*, London: Routledge, 2002, pp. 185–212.

Chapter 12

1   *PI*, 118. This relates to Wittgenstein's famous, and oft-misunderstood remark, that 'Philosophy . . . leaves everything as it is' (*PI*, 124), a remark sometimes seen, quite wrongly, as justifying a political and social quietism. Rather, one understands this remark properly by emphasising both philosophy (i.e., '*Philosophy* leaves everything as it is'—but politics, or science, or earthquakes, most certainly do not) and 'everything' (i.e., 'philosophy leaves *everything* as it is'—both attempts to change the world *and* attempts to stop it changing). But in addition, as Pleasants notes, 'Wittgenstein's way of looking at things really does "leave . . . everything as it is" . . . But it also . . . *changes* everything, for it can, as he says, change the way we look at things': Nigel Pleasants, 'A critical use of Marx and Wittgenstein', in G. Kitching and N. Pleasants (eds), *Marx and Wittgenstein: Knowledge, Morality and Politics*, London: Routledge, 2002, pp. 160–81. See also T.P. Uschanov, 'Ernest Gellner's criticisms of Wittgenstein and ordinary language philosophy', in G. Kitching and N. Pleasants (eds), *Marx and Wittgenstein: Knowledge, Morality and Politics*, London: Routledge, 2002, pp. 38–9. There are in fact important parallels in Wittgenstein's later philosophy both with *Gestalt* psychology and with Marx's early philosophy, and especially the famous eleventh *Thesis on Feuerbach* ('Philosophers have only interpreted the world in

various ways, the thing however is to change it'). Wittgenstein would endorse Marx's thesis to an extent—i.e., to the extent of agreeing that if you wish to change the world, philosophising about it will not, in and of itself, be of any assistance.

2   The interwar and immediate postwar theorists of the so-called 'Frankfurt School' specialised in this kind of analysis. For two good accounts see Martin Jay, *The Dialectical Imagination: A History of the Frankfurt School and the Institute of Social Research 1923–1950*, Boston: Little-Brown, 1973; and for the ideological aspect of their thought in particular, Raymond Geuss, *The Idea of a Critical Theory: Habermas and the Frankfurt School*, Cambridge: Cambridge University Press, 1981.

3   In a letter to Franz Mehring, written in July 1893. See *Marx-Engels Selected Works in One Volume*, London: Lawrence & Wishart, 1968, p. 690.

4   Perhaps the classical text of this type is Georg Lukács, *History and Class Consciousness*, London: Merlin Press, 1971, most especially the essays 'Class consciousness' and 'Reification and the consciousness of the proletariat', pp. 46–82 and 83–222. The original German edition of the book was published in 1922.

5   For a popular account of Wittgenstein's commitment to this view and of a confrontational debate between Wittgenstein and another great philosopher who denied it—Karl Popper—see David Edmonds and John Eidinow, *Wittgenstein's Poker: The Story of a Ten-Minute Argument Between Two Great Philosophers*, London: HarperCollins, 2001.

Bibliography

Ackerman, R.J., *Wittgenstein's City*, Amherst: University of Massachusetts Press, 1988

Althusser, L., *For Marx*, London: Verso, 1977

——*Lenin and Philosophy and Other Essays*, London: New Left Books, 1977

——*The Future Lasts Forever: A Memoir*, New York: New Press, 1993

Althusser, L. and Balibar, E., *Reading Capital*, London: New Left Books, 1970

Austin, John, *How to Do Things with Words*, Oxford: Oxford University Press, 1965

Bagehot, Walter, *The English Constitution*, London: Fontana/Collins, 1963

Benton, Ted, *The Rise and Fall of Structural Marxism: Althusser and His Influence*, London: Macmillan, 1984

Cavell, Stanley, *The Claim of Reason: Wittgenstein, Skepticism, Morality and Tragedy*, Oxford: Oxford University Press, 1979

Crary, A. and Read, R. (eds), *The New Wittgenstein*, London: Routledge, 2000

Dawkins, Richard, *The God Delusion*, London: Bantam, 2006

Drury, M.O'C., 'Some Notes on Conversations with Wittgenstein', in Rush Rhees (ed.), *Recollections of Wittgenstein*, Oxford: Oxford University Press, 1984, pp. 76–171

Edmonds, David and Eidinow, John, *Wittgenstein's Poker: The Story of a Ten-Minute Argument Between Two Great Philosophers*, London: HarperCollins, 2001

Elliott, Gregory, *Althusser: The Detour of Theory*, London: Verso, 1987

Foucault, Michel, *The Archeology of Knowledge*, London: Tavistock, 1972

——'What is Enlightenment', in P. Rabinow (ed.), *The Foucault Reader*, New York: Pantheon Books, 1984, pp. 32–50

Gasking, P.A.T. and Jackson, A.C., 'Wittgenstein as Teacher', in K.T. Fann (ed.), *Ludwig Wittgenstein: The Man and His Philosophy*, New York: Dell, 1967

Gay, Peter, *The Enlightenment: An Interpretation* (2 volumes): Volume 2, *The Science of Freedom*, London: Weidenfeld & Nicolson, 1970

Geuss, Raymond, *The Idea of a Critical Theory: Habermas and the Frankfurt School*, Cambridge: Cambridge University Press, 1981

Giddens, Anthony, 'Reason without Revolution? Habermas's *Theorie die kommunikativen Handelns*', in Richard J. Bernstein (ed.), *Habermas and Modernity*, Cambridge: Polity, 1985, pp. 95–121

Habermas, Jurgen, *Theory of Communicative Action*, Volume 1, Boston: Beacon Press, 1984

——'Questions and counterquestions', in Richard J. Bernstein (ed.), *Habermas and Modernity*, Cambridge: Polity, 1985, pp. 192–216

Hobson, John, *The Eastern Origins of Western Civilisation*, Cambridge: Cambridge University Press, 2004

Hutchinson, Phil and Read, Rupert, 'Whose Wittgenstein?', in *Philosophy*, vol. 80, 2005, pp. 432–55

Jay, Martin, *The Dialectical Imagination: A History of the Frankfurt School and the Institute of Social Research 1923–1950*, Boston: Little-Brown, 1973

Kant, Immanuel, 'What is Enlightenment?' [1784], in Isaac Kramnick (ed.), *The Portable Enlightenment Reader*, New York: Viking, 1995

Kitching, Gavin, *Karl Marx and the Philosophy of Praxis*, London: Routledge, 1988

——*Marxism and Science: Analysis of an Obsession*, University Park: Penn State Press, 1994, pp. 62–102

——*Wittgenstein and Society: Essays in Conceptual Puzzlement*, Aldershot: Ashgate, 2003

Koestler, Arthur, *The Sleepwalkers*, Harmondsworth: Penguin, 1964

Kolakowski, Leszek, 'Karl Marx and the Classical Definition of Truth', in Leszek Kolakowski, *Marxism and Beyond*, London: Paladin, 1969, pp. 59–87

Kramnick, Isaac (ed.), *The Portable Enlightenment Reader*, New York: Viking, 1995

Kremer, Michael, 'On the Purpose of Tractarian Nonsense', *Noûs*, vol. 35, no. 1, 2001, pp. 39–73

Lukács, Georg, 'Class Consciousness' and 'Reification and the Consciousness of the Proletariat', in Georg Lukács, *History and Class Consciousness*, London: Merlin Press, 1971, pp. 46–82 and 83–222

Marx, Karl and Engels, Friedrich, *Marx-Engels Selected Works in One Volume*, London: Lawrence and Wishart, 1968

Monk, Ray, *Wittgenstein: The Duty of Genius*, London: Jonathan Cape, 1990

Needham, Joseph, *Science and Civilisation in China*, Cambridge: Cambridge University Press, 1956–2004

Ostrow, M.B., *Wittgenstein's Tractatus: A Dialectical Interpretation*, Cambridge: Cambridge University Press, 2002

Pleasants, Nigel, *Wittgenstein and the Idea of a Critical Social Theory: A Critique of Giddens, Habermas and Bhaskar*, London: Routledge, 1999

——'A Critical Use of Marx and Wittgenstein', in G. Kitching and N. Pleasants (eds), *Marx and Wittgenstein: Knowledge, Morality and Politics*, London: Routledge, 2002, pp. 160–81

Porter, Roy, *The Creation of the Modern World: The Untold Story of the British Enlightenment*, New York: Norton, 2000

Racevkis, Karlis, *Postmodernism and the Search for Enlightenment*, Charlottesville: University of Virginia Press, 1993

Rorty, R. (ed.), *The Linguistic Turn: Essays in Philosophical Method*, Chicago: University of Chicago Press, 1967

Rossi-Landi, F., 'Toward a Marxian Use of Wittgenstein', in G. Kitching and N. Pleasants (eds), *Marx and Wittgenstein: Knowledge, Morality and Politics*, London: Routledge, 2002, pp. 185–212

Rubinstein, David, *Marx and Wittgenstein: Social Praxis and Social Explanation*, London: Routledge & Kegan Paul, 1981

Searle, John, *Speech Acts*, Cambridge: Cambridge University Press, 1969

Sokal, A. and Bricmont, J., *Intellectual Impostures: Postmodern Philosophers' Abuse of Science*, London: Profile Books, 1998

Stretton, Hugh, *The Political Sciences*, London: Routledge & Kegan Paul, 1969

Uschanov, T.P., 'Ernest Gellner's criticisms of Wittgenstein and ordinary language philosophy', in G. Kitching and N. Pleasants (eds), *Marx and Wittgenstein: Knowledge, Morality and Politics,* London: Routledge, 2002, pp. 23–46

Winch, Peter, *The Idea of a Social Science and its Relation to Philosophy*, 2nd edition, London: Routledge & Kegan Paul, 1990

Wittgenstein, Ludwig, *Philosophical Investigations*, Oxford: Basil Blackwell, 1953

——*Tractatus Logico-Philosophicus*, London: Routledge & Kegan Paul, 1961

——*The Blue and Brown Books: Preliminary Studies for the 'Philosophical Investigations'*, Oxford: Basil Blackwell, 1969

——*Culture and Value*, Oxford: Basil Blackwell, 1980

——*Zettel* (2nd edition), Oxford: Basil Blackwell, 1981

Wokler, Robert, 'The Enlightenment Project and its Critics', in S.E. Liedman (ed.), 'The Postmodernist Critique of the Project of Enlightenment', *Poznam Studies in The Philosophy of the Sciences and the Humanities*, vol. lviii, 1998, pp. 13–30

Index